Love Will Out

Dear Marion,

A little thankyou from the NEAC S for enabling us to have a carefree weekend away.

With love,
David Marcus

Dedication

To Glynne Evans, Jean Woods and all
those longsuffering CMS staff members
past and present who helped these
letters to appear.

Love Will Out

*A Theology of Mission for today's world:
CMS newsletters 1975–85*

Rt. Rev. Simon Barrington-Ward

Marshall Pickering

Marshall Morgan and Scott
Marshall Pickering
3 Beggarwood Lane, Basingstoke, Hants RG23 7LP, UK

British Library CIP Data

Barrington-Ward, Simon
  Love will out.
  1. Mission of the church
  I. Title
  266   BV601.8

ISBN 0-551-01599-3

Text set in Century Textbook by Brian Robinson, Buckingham
Printed in Great Britain by Richard Clay Ltd, Bungay, Suffolk

Contents

Contents

Part III   Christ For The World

Introduction

Sometimes, at the end of the day, through what may seem to have been a random succession of events, you can discern a definite pattern emerging.

That's what I feel as I look through this collection of fragmentary pieces. I'm certain that, almost to my own surprise, a coherent theme has been weaving itself through the whole sequence, over ten years. Gradually, looking back, I begin to see them more and more as a set of variations. The theme itself an interplay, a fusion of opposites. It is a constant coming together of Heaven and Earth, universal and particular, divine and human, judgement and mercy, spiritual and material, ideal and reality, structure and community, joy and sorrow, in a whole range of varied contexts.

In the melting pot of our present world, I seem to have kept glimpsing it again, this final bringing into one of the Creator and the creation in the crucified figure of Jesus Christ, disclosing Himself through the Spirit.

I think this divine interweaving first found definite embodiment for me when I was giving a talk at breakfast, rather to my horror, in the presence of both my predecessors, Canon Max Warren and Bishop John Taylor. The Breakfast was one of those magnificent institutions which came out of the remotest antiquity of CMS and still had a valuable contemporary function. It brought together a formidable range of august friends, representatives of partner bodies and senior counsellors of the Society. So it had a rather dream-like character, but I am quite clear that I was very much awake at the time. With the portraits of at least two of those present hanging on the very walls of 157, the house where we were met, and the guests below them all gazing, I was talking about faces. You will find the piece called 'Point of Balance' on page 106. I spoke about the 'right human face' as Edwin Muir called it. Already as I had prepared the talk I had seen the characteristic of that right or true face as being a 'juxta-position of opposed qualities'. I mean not only a blend of sternness and tenderness, or shrewdness and innocence, but behind these strange interrelations, a holding in one of infinite and finite, of that sublimely eternal presence which ultimately encompasses everything being contained, and wholly con-tained, in a particular place and movement and moment. But suddenly then and there, at the breakfast table, I knew that this sacramental reality is latent in everyone, and is what everyone is looking for, today more than ever before. It is the informing and infusing of the mere, ragged, every-day trivial surface detail of life, with a depth and universality which gives our confused, contemporary struggles eternal meaning. To grasp it is to recognise how all our conflicting inter-pretations of life, economic, sociological and metaphysical, in fact intermesh.

Each sees only a part of what is a continuing redemptive process, everlastingly at work, or at least till the end of time. And we only truly perceive its source, its theme and its goal when the glory of God is revealed to us in the face of Jesus Christ.

Now this interrelation, which appeared of itself, like that, so early in my time at CMS, has continued to unfold ever since and has not yet exhausted its meaning by any means for me, nor ever shall.

I rejoice that there are many variations yet to come. And so I dare to hope that those who will look back with me through these pages over the encounters of ten years, will also glimpse with me, some of the many ways in which, in the seeming confusion and disintegration of our day, 'all things hold together in Christ'. (Colossians 1:17)

Simon Barrington-Ward
The Bishop's House
Coventry   November 1987

PART I

The Personal Centre

The Personal Centre

Why interfere with the beliefs of people of other faiths and cultures? This is a question which would seem to confront missionary-minded Christians with increasing force. Our present world is justifiably suspicious of any activity that savours of the domination or the manipulation of others or that carries any suggestion of our imposing our own beliefs and opinions uninvited upon others. There is justifiably a widespread revulsion against the insensitive arrogance of the West.

In such a mood some Christian theologians have been concerned to carry through a re-evaluation of many of the assumptions and claims of Christians to a point at which they have begun seriously to doubt the propriety of Christian missionary efforts. Not long ago on television a couple of them agreed that such imperialistic ventures were now outdated. We had entered upon an era of exploratory synthesis between all faiths.

When suave politeness, tempering bigot zeal,
Corrected 'I believe' to 'one does feel ...'
(Ronald Knox, *Absolute and A Bit of Hell*)

As the two were speaking, one sensed the gulf that must be opening up between them and those ordinary church members who were viewing them from afar. Not only that; the same gulf might appear even to run through the heart and mind and practice of such theologians themselves. They seemed to be stretched, with what must surely sometimes be a rather uncomfortable flexibility, between the points at which they preach and pray.

All Christians must become aware of this same kind of tension at moments. How do they respond when they meet with the rich moral and spiritual resources of those of other patterns of belief and worship? How far can we be truly conscious of the unique universality of Jesus Christ and yet open to the wealth of beauty and insight in the spirituality and thought of those who do not acknowledge him as Lord? Is it even possible to envisage that very wealth of 'the nations' being brought into the very light of 'the Lamb', the crucified Christ, in that final city of God whose gates are never to be shut?

Let God be God
The answer may begin to be found when we turn away from ourselves to experience some of the tensions encountered—and resolved—by others. For instance, take a young Muslim scholar a few years ago facing an uproar in a conference of his fellow believers as he expounds to them the argument of his thesis on the Qur'an. His unpopular case is that they must go back behind many of the assumptions of traditional Islam to what the holy Book actually said in its historical context. He calls them to break with the sophisticated pronouncements of later Islamic philosophers about the inscrutable unknowable God and turn to the simple concrete directness of the Prophet's original vision. Muhammad was concerned only to proclaim judgment on all idolatry and on the immoral way of life that it generated. The Qur'an, our young scholar bravely maintained, has been mis-read and misinterpreted by Muslims in the light of later social and intellectual preoccupations.

If you read the Qur'an freshly and directly there is no trace of the arbitrary incomprehensible God of later Islamic philosophy, decreeing his all-predestining will. The 'infinite pattern of the arabesques of Islamic art,' to quote a recent commentator, 'speaks eloquently of no individual, no unit, no person, no historical event but rather of the eternal transcendent unity, that pure and lovely and lonely world view of Sunni Islam at its most sublime.'

But, so the young critic argued, this is all a later heritage.

The Qur'an itself, the pre-theological, pre-Greek, Arabic book, is a very different matter. Its over-riding theme, he maintained, in almost every sura, is the living God, the strict Judge, punishing the sinner, loving the penitent and guiltless and evoking fear and awe, utterly ethical and moral, the righteous one leaping out of those decorative pages and demanding our obedient response. The uproar that followed, the cries of 'withdraw', were simply a reaction against any criticism of the tradition, any attempt to get back behind to an original content.

It had a strange effect upon the speaker. In some way this rejection by his people of what he knew to be true, forced him back into a lonely exploration of the very truth he had been expounding. Some observers felt he might be being driven further than he knew. And so indeed it proved. Wrestling against the seeming hostility of others to his theme of the righteousness of God, he found himself, to his own surprise, to his own cost, being steadily pressed back towards the Cross. Painful as it was to be for him, destructive indeed of his very being, he began to feel the facts closing in upon him. He began to sense the central necessity of Jesus and his Cross to his very exposition of the Qur'an. If, he argued, God is truly righteous; if, as the Prophet commanded, we are truly to let God be God and his righteousness be revealed in a world of tragedy and suffering and moral failure, there is only one way in which this can happen. There is only one way in which a fully personal and truly just God, such as Muhammad proclaimed, can realise his purpose in such a world as this. That is, by himself bearing the suffering of the world and the consequences of our transgression. How can he be the just God of the Qur'an unless, in total innocence, he suffers more than any man?

This is the only way in which his justice can be realised, and his compassion and his righteousness meet perfectly. So for the young Muslim thinker, as he struggles with the Qur'an itself, the figure of Jesus springs into the centre, the wounded Man in the heavens becomes the fulfilment of the inner logic of the Qur'anic revelation. God becomes God in deed. We are back to Romans itself, and the struggle to understand the fully consistent nature of divine justice throws the seeker back upon God in Christ crucified and risen.

The spiritual quest for the centre

There is, it seems to me, a great deal to be teased out of this story. First, there is the effort towards the rediscovery of the Personal God in the Qur'an, the God of whom the Prophet himself was speaking. This young scholar's move in this direction was part of a much wider move towards the Personal within many faiths today, which has its own precedents in the history of each.

It is a striking fact that the more impersonal abstract metaphysical patterns of faith have often been supported by the establishment, while the non-conformists or the more marginal people in the society have tended to break with the forms that surround them and search for a more personal communion with God and with each other. In the end sometimes a balance is reached, as in Islam, with Al-Ghazali arriving at a balance between Sufism and the orthodox framework. But it's a tension, it's a struggle within the great faiths. We find in Hinduism the more impersonal orthodoxy which was Shankara's system, classical Hinduism, being confronted in a kind of social upheaval with a reform movement which led to Bhakti, to the ecstatic communion with a single personal god behind the gods. We find the growing popularity of the Bhagavadgita has made it increasingly central for many Hindus, again achieving some sort of a balance, perhaps, between the two.

And the same could be said of Mahayana Buddhism and the Lotus sutra with its intense concentration on the person of the Buddha, going with an upheaval and a stirring within Buddhism of the same kind. Robin Horton has pointed out how frequently in African religions the more private personalised cults of the free spirits of the wild or the water are in contrast with the official central cult of the fathers or the founders, and are more intimate and personal, often belonging to inferior people in the society. In the history of

Christendom itself there has been the continuously recurrent theme of struggle against legalism and formalism, together with a searching for a rediscovery of liberating personal grace.

Everywhere it has been the same story—a weakening of the formal social framework makes room for a greater discovery of the Personal in God and a freer relationship between people that goes with it. Again and again such movements have provided the bridge, the point of entry, not surprisingly, for the Christian gospel into other faiths. In Islam it has been the eccentrics in search of a more fully and intimately personal God who have found Jesus. It is no wonder that it is in the context of the less orthodox Shi'ite Islam, with its desire to be guided by an actual living succession of Imams, that this quest for the personal in the shape of a cult of the eternal living Muhammad, has arisen most strikingly. This became the religion of Iran. And it was in Iran that, as western Europe first began to impinge on the social and political order, scattered individuals here and there began to respond one by one and so contributed to the slow growth of that astonishing phenomenon, the Christian Church in Iran. In William McElwee Miller's book *Ten Muslims meet Christ* you come across the most astonishing stories of isolated individuals who, sometimes moved by a dream or a vision or the reading of the Bible on their own, found their way to Jesus. There is Khadijeh the poetess, who picked up a Bible and studied the references to Jesus in the Qur'an; then she had a dream that she met Jesus—she was only a child at the time, and when she told her sister this she reported it to her father who wept, as he felt certain that she would one day become a Christian, and he was right. Or there is Mirza Ibrahim, the martyr of Tabriz, who found his own way again to such a faith that he was ready to be beaten and kicked and strangled by fellow-prisoners in the end, saying 'Jesus is true, choke me if you will'. Or there are extraordinary characters like the famous Mansur, bookseller and dispenser, a fiery, magnetic figure, who travelled round Iran, always changing his hat and his garb after some fresh discovery of Christ or some fresh understanding of himself, and growing yearly more like John the Baptist. Or Jahil Quarzal, the schoolmaster who taught the exiled Bishop of Iran, Bishop Hassan Deqhani Tafti. He was an incredible man, drawn by the person of Christ and bringing to Christ all his marvellous penmanship and poetry famous among Muslims in Iran, and at his death winning a poem from one of the greatest Irani poets in celebration of his gifts.

All of them are drawn to the same central Person, just in the way Bishop Hassan describes in his own autobiography *Design of my World*, as the stumbling block becomes the stepping stone. It is that personal communion that attracts. In India perhaps it was supremely Bhakti which made the bridge for many to the mind and the imagination. It has been well said by an Indian commentator that 'India will give its heart to Christ before it gives its head'. The poets and the mystics themselves crossed the bridge of Bhakti into this more personal world, discovering the personal communion with Christ. Men like the great Narayan Tilak, poet of Maharashtra, who started just by being given the New Testament in the train and developed to the point where he became a Christian *sannyasi* or holy man seeking for, as he put it, 'Christ in his naked beauty, free from the disguise of western organisation, western doctrines, and western forms of worship'. A great wealth of Christian Bhakti poetry remains to be explored and translated in a more attractive form than it is at present, where it reads too much like the poorer bits of Ancient and Modern. It could be retranslated wonderfully.

Sundar Singh himself was reared as 'bhakti' as well as a Sikh, another personalist movement, and as a small boy learnt the Bhagavadgita by heart. He searched the Upanishads and even the Qur'an and he practised Yoga without assuaging his despair of finding a personal God. As he said himself, he was led to think of suicide, of casting himself on the railway lines, before that morning on which he was surprised, walking behind the houses of his home-town in Patiala, by a vision of Jesus, radiant in his beauty, and commanding the obedience that led him to a life of wandering all over India.

In Nigeria I knew a number of prophets and prophetesses linked to local Christian movements, who were quite evidently the direct heirs of the nature spirit cults in their areas, but who had found in Jesus the fulfilment of their quest for a fully personal and universal power. One healer said to me, 'Previously when I was possessed I knew something already of what I have now known completely in Jesus himself'. They felt that they were touching on the source of a new cleansing strength, of new relationships, of a new understanding of human nature itself. They had found a transformation of their lives which was reflected in their faces. In East Africa, at an even greater moral depth, I believe we see in the continuous succession of spiritual movements, a search for a personal relatedness to God and to one another, which people have been touching upon in their discovery of Jesus and his Cross. There also is a vast, still unrealised potential in that grasping out for the personal Christ. The same is true in the Church of the Southern Sudan marked as it is with the profound growth in the realisation of Christ that came about in the refuge of the forest during the civil war.

In the Northern Sudan, a Sudanese friend in Khartoum once remarked to me, 'the young are looking for God to be with them as a friend. They are hungry for personal communion'—that was the phrase of one who had struggled his way from Islam to Christ by way of membership of the Muslim Brotherhood and through an extraordinary story of incidents. There is a sense in which God is shaking together and shaking out old patterns and frameworks, not just here but all over the world, and as he does so new cults, new spiritual openings spread among the young and social change carries with it a far more widespread quest than ever before for a more personalised spirituality.

So I think that was one of the things that our young Muslim thinker was feeling for as he wrestled with the Qur'an.

The humanist quest for the centre
A second thing that I think he was feeling for is a very different sort of movement which also points to the personal,

and that is the spread of certain universally shared values. When he said that God, the just God, must share the injustices of this world, must suffer in this world, he was predicating of God some kind of a sense of justice, of humane justice, which he himself had freshly discovered, perhaps which he himself was realising in a new way. As the cities into which great multitudes of the world are moving spread, as the urban consciousness spreads and as the old collective views of the world are being undermined, they bring with them a new loneliness, a new freedom, a new disturbance and promise like that which was registered by those Iranians or by Sundar Singh. They bring with them not only the economic frustration, the multiplying bustees or slums, they bring with them new quests.

These quests may be experienced certainly spiritually by the more sensitive in dreams and visions, in a new interpretation of a Holy Book or in the new discovery of Jesus. The first tremors may have been sensed by those movements that reached out for Christ even from within Islam itself long ago in pre-British days in the north of Nigeria or as in certain new pentecostal movements like the little tiny new Church in Kashmir. But there is also a spread with this disturbance of more common personal values, which some people speak of as having become more universal than any faith, a kind of general humanism, a humane conspiracy, if you like. It often seems to exist over against the establishment that surrounds it, a modernisation, a sense of human dignity and need, sometimes felt passionately by the frustrated and the powerless, sometimes issuing in a fervent utopianism. If it becomes communist it will always be communist with a human face. It can, in a rarer setting, sometimes even be capitalist with a human face. It's a quest for the Personal, for a mercy that

> . . . has a human heart,
> Pity a human face,
> And love the human form divine,
> And peace the human dress.
> (William Blake, 'The Divine Image', *Songs of Innocence and Experience*)

As the cultural frameworks of the past fall away, men are left naked in their needs and yearnings, and in an epoch of unique danger and unique opportunity, there is what Macmurray long ago called 'the crisis of the Personal'. There is here a philosophy, a faith, that perhaps is increasingly required—that is demanded by and accompanies sometimes democracy and science and technology and many other western ideas—indeed it is something which at its finest I believe is the fruit of the West and I believe goes back to the whole Judaeo-Christian tradition, and again to the Person of Jesus himself. Everywhere it seems to me the poets and the novelists of all faiths are alive with this quest of which in the West perhaps Chaucer and Shakespeare were the pioneers and the great nineteenth- and twentieth-century novelists the supreme exemplars.

Look, for instance, at T. K. Thomas's beautiful surveys of Indian novels and short stories opening up the passionate commitment of the writers to the human, in whatever form they express it, a passionate concern for the God of justice perhaps, or is it an ironic humanism in Ismat Chugtai's Urdu story *Tina's Granny*, the story of an old woman who, as he describes her, 'lives on garbage and gossip', a tale-bearer, a cheat a liar living unloved and uncared for. And these are the ironic words with which the story ends:

> On judgment day the trumpet sounded, and granny woke with a start and got up coughing and clearing her throat, as though her ears had caught the sound of free food being doled out. . . . Cursing and swearing at the angels, she dragged herself somehow or other, doubled up as she was, over the Bridge of Sirat and burst into the presence of God the All powerful and All kind . . . and God, beholding the degradation of humanity, bowed his head in shame and wept tears of blood [which] fell upon the rough grave and bright red poppies sprang up there and began to dance in the breeze.

How very near we are, in a very different world of feeling, much more Hindu and much more ironic, how very near we are nonetheless to the affirmation of our Muslim scholar that the God of justice must himself suffer. For Nayantara Sahgal the Bible and Christian faith are often in her novels implicit as a critique of Indian society. In many of the other novels and stories which Thomas explores as well the same humane values are being expressed. The writers are not of course concerned with religious doctrines. They are concerned with people with no categories to qualify them. They are concerned simply with the human predicament, the wretchedness, the helplessness, the possibilities of human compassion and forgiveness. Basic human responsibility for one's neighbour is no longer to be dodged, no longer to be laid at the door of the gods. All that is left is simple human justice, as in that searching poem of a modern Indian writer:

> On that day
> the simple men will come
> those who had no place
> in the books and poems
> of the intellectuals
> but delivered daily
> their bread and milk
> their tortillas and eggs
> those who mended their clothes
> those who drove their cars
> those who cared for their dogs
> and worked in their gardens;
> and they'll ask:
> What did you do when the poor
> suffered, when tenderness and life
> burned out in them?[1]

The gods are fading, the rituals and traditions are failing younger people. They are breaking with all conformity, defying the conventional, the virtuous and the pharisaical. Humbugs and hypocrites are bitterly exposed. Even Gandhiism has lost its spell and this India does not have any mystical answers, only human self-sacrifice and simple caring. T. K. Thomas notes a striking saying of Scott, an American critic: 'a secular literature like this may have a profoundly religious function to perform. For by the very resolvedness with which it may plunge us into the dark it may precipitate us out of our forgetfulness, so that our very deprivation of the transcendent may bring us close to its mystery.' These writings, he suggests, have in them many of the elements of prayer. 'They are more than a preparation for prayer, they are themselves a kind of prayer.'

Perhaps our best guide both to the negations and to the affirmations of this humanist literature which is multiplying in all cultures is Wole Soyinka, the greatest African writer now working in English, I believe. I shall never forget the vivid impact of *Dance of the Forest*, his great play for Nigerian independence, on my first evening in Nigeria at the birth of a new nation. It was not just the wonderful rich play of language, it was not just the genuinely West African English of lyrical power nor the mastery of a whole new idiom. It was the complexity, the tragic sense, the irony, the feeling for human frailty with which the traditional images and rhythms were tempered. Here was a restatement of African religions and philosophy in humanist terms. The ancestors return to a feast of their descendants only to reveal the same tensions and limitations that their present descendants have. There is a disillusionment; even courage and integrity are mistaken and not always enough. A painful expiation has to be wrought out, bringing a reconciliation between men and God, and a half-child which has been born of the dead has to be released—it seems hauntingly to foreshadow Nigeria's own future travail. There is a tragic sense, already, at that moment of rejoicing.

Nonetheless the earlier plays of Soyinka were in the main witty, comic explorations of some Nigerian predicaments with an underlying feeling for the need to recover an essentially realistic and humane social tradition which he believed was truly African. I don't think he really acknowledged how many other ingredients there were here. It was at the very least a thoroughgoing re-interpretation of

African tradition, but it did have, as for instance his brilliant Africanised version of the *Bacchae*, a certain zest, a richness which he drew directly from his Yoruba tradition. It was a subtle and urbane variation on a theme, his wonderful exploration, for instance of a fraudulent prophet on the beach at Lagos in *The Trials of Brother Jero*.

But it took the closing in of civil war and personal suffering in the form of imprisonment to etch the shadows more deeply and to establish the promise of greatness. *Kongi's Harvest*, his next play, sees the pathetic pretensions of a new political order bitterly exposed. And then Brother Jero, the prophet himself, becomes a sinister instrument of an amoral regime with public executions. *Madmen and Specialists* is an almost macabre, fiercely despairing play. It lacks the proportion, perhaps, of that remarkable testimony that Soyinka himself wrote from his civil war experience *A Man Died*. As a reviewer put it, 'The man dies who keeps silent in the face of tyranny'—and that was very much the theme of the book. Here in the Nigerian setting, Soyinka catches up another great universal theme of the humanism of our time. It is the theme of the free and sovereign victim defying and breaking the captivity of the system. Doctorowsky's *Book of Daniel* and Solzhenitsyn's whole opus, plays of Lumumba's death, *The Trial of Beyers Naude*, the legend of Dubček and even more of Jan Palach, and more recently, I think, the story and film, *One Flew over the Cuckoo's Nest*. There is a universal passion play abroad in one version or another.

Soyinka's *A Shuttle in the Crypt*, his poems, echoes the same mood in verse, never more resonant than in his staggering requiem for a condemned man in his prison, hanged just near his cell.

> Into this last turning, pilgrim,
> Turn alone and bid you welcome
> Into this last kingdom, king,
> Priest and subject.

Christianity, or at least the Christian Church in various

guises, fares ill in Soyinka's writings, as in many of the Indian stories. But perhaps it is significant that in a large-scale fantasy, his second novel, *Season of Anomy*, a description of the collapse of a society exploited by big business and military power, the springs of regeneration are found in a community. This hidden commune, Aiyero, isolated from the society, is a source of humane conspiracy and affirmation in the face of cruelty and horror. It is dedicated to African religious values, of course immediately recalling Aiyetoro, the Christian community which Charles Tett has so wonderfully described for us. Wole Soyinka cannot allow his version to be Christian. This would still be paying 'lip service', as he says in the book, to a white god, a dubious god, the bearers of whose faith 'kill, burn, maim, loot and enslave our people'. But yet the only actual living source of the kind of humanism he stands for is in fact in this book modelled on a Christian community, and, significantly, one which is an indigenous discovery of Christ. Aiyetoro, a Christian utopia, has perhaps lost something of its first shining promise. But it is still today nonetheless a very fascinating group of people, a Christian growth on the shores of Nigeria. And there Soyinka finds at least the springs, the possibilities, of an African rebirth.

A wounded Man in the heavens
I see a pressure gradually building up, in scattered places, here concentrated, there diffused, fragmentary, ambiguous and yet taken as a whole I believe unmistakable, towards the person of the crucified and risen Christ, the personal God. There is a universal search for One who is truly personal. The story of the young Muslim scholar with which I began is characteristic of this search. And perhaps the most striking feature of his story is the clear insistence that it is God himself—the Judge of all the earth—who must be the One who bears our suffering. The central passion must be the passion of God himself. There can be no true relationship between man and a personal God unless God himself becomes human and suffers. All other conceptions of union with God, whether mystical, by some kind of self-

transcendence, or moral, by some kind of legalistic obedience, carry with them some kind of illusion. They conceal the essential, glaring discontinuity between our tragically bounded life and the limitless free life of God. Whoever it may be—the young Muslim scholar, Sundar Singh the African prophet, my Sudanese friend, Bishop Hassan—they all alike discover in Jesus that God was in Christ and in him it is the overcoming of the tragic destiny of all men, and of themselves among them, that they meet with.

As F. D. Maurice wrote once to his unitarian father, he found in Jesus God meeting him as a friend. And not only as a friend but as One who could meet within him his own failures, One who in his suffering was truly with him and for him.

It is just this mode of relationship with the divine for which people in so many cultures and places are alike looking. And it is precisely the kind of human society which expresses this relationship for which they yearn.

Now the tragedy of the kind of theology which we might seem to be offering them, if those television screen theologians were to be believed, is that just at the moment when people are most hungry for 'God with us', some of our own theologians have been doing their best to dismantle what they obviously conceive to be such a problematic notion. They have made a procrustean bed for themselves out of their own categories, and they twist this way and that to fit their theology into it. In the 60s they tended to Christianity without God; in the 70s they turned to Christianity without Christ; in the 80s they disintegrated Christianity itself. The undermining, the destruction of the union of Jesus himself with God, the taking apart of the Trinitarian heart of our faith, is really an attempt to remove the very personal ground for which people everywhere are searching. As St Thomas declared, speaking of the Trinity, 'persona est relatio', the personal consists in relatedness. It is that relationship between the divine and human by which we are enabled to share the very life of God himself. It is in the very establishment of that relationship at infinite cost, that Jesus is unique, is distinctive, is of universal significance to men of all faiths or none. He is able to bring forgiveness and reconciliation to mystic and moralist, to the spiritually and the humanistically minded alike.

We are privileged to be participating in our time in a universal crisis, a turning point in history in which human beings all over the world are feeling for a new sense of personal being. It is a description of when times are ripe, it is a moment for a vision of a wounded Man in the heavens.

But what we require above all at such a time is confidence in him, patience, sensitivity, the ability to listen before we speak, a deep closeness to Christ, a deep closeness to the poor, an expectancy and a vigilance that is ready to wait and let the Spirit flow; to 'let the seed grow secretly' in ways that will surprise us. Essentially Jesus will dawn in each culture in his own way at his own time in the consciousness of each place and people. We are only, together with those who look to his coming in each place, preparing, and trying not to be glaring obstacles in the process. In a new sense of St Paul's words we are labouring 'until Christ be formed' in each particular thought and feeling world. Every culture including our own has to be broken, has to go through its own repentance and change. And must wait.

My wise Sudanese Christian friend said from his Muslim background that 'in the Sudan there is a latent faith, a latent Christ, a latent Church. I do not believe you will find it in the Church as it is now'. And a missionary wrote to me from the Middle East the other day:

I sometimes wonder whether in God's grace the conversion of the House of Islam may not come from established Churches at all. It may even be that many of the Churches will continue their present path to the logical conclusion of ultimate extinction. But with Islam itself I think there may be a Christian stirring of the pulse —I seem to sense it. Isn't it just possible that the witness for instance of the deaf and other handicapped Muslims who have reached to Christ might be a means of a magnetic attraction and revelation? I think I see it happening, just as to doubting Thomas the Lord was revealed through his wounds, maybe he will also be revealed to Islam through his contemporary wounds, the deaf and the handicapped for whom the Eastern world generally has little space.

That is one tiny sign of a universal sense of quickening, as he puts it, a stirring of the pulse, a shift in society which calls for a shift in the apprehension of God and of man all over the world. Perhaps there are crucial choices to be made if men are to find the springs of their humanity in a crucified and living God.

The seed grows secretly and one is amazed again and again to find the latent Christ flashing out as Lord of some new world, whether it be among the Maasai women dancing with their Pastor and singing their praise songs in Kenya as they bring those songs into the Church, or whether it be when you pick up Shusaku Endo's novel *Wonderful Fool* and see a Japanese Christ.

One thing is clear from the spiritual quest and the humanist quest alike toward the Personal, that the present form of the Church is an obstacle. All the people I have described renounce it in one way or another, perhaps by wandering, perhaps by detaching themselves from the Churches, perhaps by criticising and exposing them. But it has always been the lot of the Church to be an obstacle. Even Augustine found it so. And yet we must long for this readiness to wait for new forms to emerge, to feel for a fresh, simple, flexible way of being Christ in the world, which surely has so much to say about the reshaping of the Church. And places like Aiyetoro, or the Jesus Family in China in the past, or the present movements like some Pentecostal communities and Churches of the poor in South America or the Philippines, Ernesto Cardinale's island community off Latin America—all these things point to some kind of Church that perhaps the Third World is discerning more clearly than we can, a Church that could rise to Wole Soyinka's expectations, where he says in his admiration for Aiyero, the mythical community: 'They live by an idea, I believe they will suffer without being corrupted or swayed.'

'I have argued then that they do indeed live by an idea whose hour has come. In the true Aiyetoro, it is more than an idea—it is a relationship, a relatedness to God's life and to each other in the crucified One. And it is in the demonstration of this relatedness, the sharing of this conviction, that the Church in its small, quiet, continuous way must bear witness afresh. And I believe that it might play a modest part in this universal process.

Recommended books

William McElwee Miller, *Ten Muslims meet Christ*, (Eerdmans, Grand Rapids, 1969).

H. Dehqani-Tafti, *Design of my world*, (Lutterworth, 1959 and 1968).

Robin Boyd, *An Introduction to Indian Christian Theology*, (Christian Literature Society, India, 1969).

Oliver Allison, *Through Fire and Water:* Ten critical years in the life of the Church in the Southern Sudan, 1964–1974, (CMS, 1976).

T. K. Thomas, articles in *Religion and Society*, vol. XIX, no. 3 (September 1972) and vol. XX. no. 4 (December 1973), and in *Bangalore Theological Forum*, vol. V, no. 2 (July–December 1973).

Wole Soyinka, *A Shuttle in the Crypt:* Poems (Rex Collings/Eyre Methuen, 1972). *The Man Died* (Rex Collings, 1973). *Collected Plays* (OUP, Oxford Paperback, 2 vols., 1973). *Season of Anomy* (Rex Collings, 1973).

Call to Prayer

It has been said that prayer is a sigh. And it is true that a heartwrung sigh is an almost involuntary yielding up of all that is in you, as if to some other being beyond you. It could be a sigh of utter content or delight or of wonder. It could be a venting of the kind of feeling E. M. Forster once described experiencing when, for all his agnosticism, he found himself wanting to thank someone or something. It could be a sigh out of an abyss of sorrow, a sigh of weariness with a life we never chose to be brought into. Such sighs go up from cities and countrysides, from comfortable villas and makeshift tents, from clusters of huts in villages, from forests or deserts, from wherever there is even the most transient human existence. The sighs of happiness and despair, they seem to go up on one great mingled exhalation.

David Fanshawe evokes a sense of this vast unconscious liturgy of all mankind's joys and griefs in his marvellous interweaving of some of the sounds and songs of Africa with the polyphony of a western choir, chanting certain parts of the mass in Latin. Perhaps the most inspired moment of his *African Sanctus*, as he calls it, is the original juxtaposition from which the whole symphony sprang. It is the point at which the composer records the Islamic call to prayer—that perpetual unearthly cry out of one of man's intensest impulses towards the divine—and then sets it beside and within the contrapuntal movement of a great hymn to Jesus as Lord, the *Kyrie Eleison*. I shall never again hear that call, nor even look at an ordinary set of slides of scenes from different aspects of the life of the family of man, without recalling at least the echo of that all-inclusive *Lord have mercy*, overarching the muezzin's vibrant tones.

There is one place, it seems to say, in and beyond the varied life of this world where all the sighs of men are brought together and all are heard together. This seems to me the essential point of collections like Constance Padwick's beautiful *Muslim Devotions*, Kenneth Cragg's *Alive unto God*, and, even more explicitly, John Carden's superb *Morning, Noon and Night*. Exultation and joy, pain and unutterable sadness, all are fused into one, and the darkness ultimately contained within the light of those all-embracing words 'through Jesus Christ'. Prayer within the shadow of his Cross, prayer touched by the still concealed radiance of his resurrection, must always bring the sigh of yearning within the stirring of a much greater sigh of grateful wonder! This is why Karl Barth ascribed purity of heart to Mozart and called him a Christian theologian, because, as he put it, 'he heard the harmony of creation to which the shadow also belongs' but in which 'shadow is not darkness ... sadness cannot become despair' and life 'does not fear death but knows it well'. He knew the Cross, at which alone prayer never becomes mere submission or detachment, looking at the world through the wrong end of a telescope from some lofty mystical height. Rather here, and here only, prayer combines in one movement both the wordless peace of communion with the God of the life to come and the most specific and urgent concern for the life of man in this present world.

Watchers on the mountain
There have always been outstanding men of prayer who themselves seemed to embody precisely this unity, not of themselves but out of their faith in Christ. It seems to have been given to them, after his likeness, to live out from day to day just this profound integration of serenity and suffering which he uniquely realised. They have come to hold together in themselves, not without great cost, such a vision of God and such compassion for men that they begin at least to become what we were all made to be, true men.

On Mount Athos in Greece, since the ninth century, only

the Orthodox monks and the frogs have kept up their
continual round of praise. It is a great crag and promontory,
which seems to jut out beyond normal human experience, far
into and above the sea, with its thick woods, rock edges, and
what seem like the monumental outlines of certain sober
figures, standing out in silhouette like the watchmen on the
walls of Jerusalem. In his *School of Prayer*, Archbishop
Anthony Bloom tells a story of one of the most significant of
these figures known as Staretz Silouan. Like all the rest he
was quiet, self-effacing. None of his contemporaries
particularly noticed him; they were surprised that so many
people came to see him. Like so many other real men of God,
like the famous Brother Lawrence, he seemed a supremely
ordinary person. The workshops of the monastery ran well
under his care. Those who asked him anything found that he
answered them out of some kind of depth they had not
expected, with great simplicity and directness. The Russian
peasants who came there as migrant workers loved him. And
he loved them and prayed for them in a profoundly quiet way.
The story goes that he prayed for one, Nicholas, who had left
his wife behind and come to earn money.

> I prayed with tears of compassion for Nicholas, for his
> young wife, for the little child, but as I was praying the
> sense of the divine presence began to grow on me and at a
> certain moment it grew so powerful that I lost sight of
> Nicholas, his wife, his child, his needs, their village, and I
> could be aware only of God, and I was drawn by the sense
> of the divine presence deeper and deeper, until, of a sudden,
> at the heart of this presence, I met the divine love holding
> Nicholas, his wife and his child and now it was with the
> love of God that I began to pray for them again, but again I
> was drawn into the deep and in the depths of this again and
> again I found the divine love for them. . . .

The secret here, and what makes this prayer distinctively
Christian, is precisely this alternation. There is a double
presence, the presence of the Personal God in Christ and the
presence of the persons of men, of the whole world of man and

all creation. There is joy in the presence of God and yet at the same time a boundless yearning for the healing and the fulfilment of all that He has made. 'Hallowed be thy name' and yet 'Thy kingdom come' ... 'Blessed be the God and Father of our Lord Jesus Christ' ... and yet 'God is my witness how I yearn for you all'. There is the thanksgiving which was expressed in the Breaking of Bread and yet the great intercession which has always accompanied that breaking. The very quality of authenticity, of innocent realism, of completeness which characterises Silouan and his fellow monks arises out of this essential integration. A brooding sadness and tenderness is contained within their clear, luminous joy.

They arrived at this through years of steady concentration on a surrender to grace, sometimes through pain and weariness, most frequently using as a means of becoming receptive the simple and continuous invocation of Jesus, often in the words of the so-called 'Jesus Prayer', *Lord Jesus Christ, have mercy on me.* As these words become part of your very breathing, they say—the expression of your commitment, your obedience, your longing and hunger for God, above all of humble and penitent seeking—then, as it were, you begin to 'tune in'. And God of his love will pour out his Spirit upon you, enabling you to 'draw the head into the heart' as they call it, and you may be given together with the gift of tears, an ability for quiet and simple contemplation, even in the midst of activity.

But it is never separated from a pleading and a yearning on behalf of the whole creation. The Spirit pushes these men, these watchers on the edge of life, right into the heart of its central turmoil, and fills their hearts with an agonising yet liberating compassion, a longing for the whole disordered universe to be transfigured by grace. They stand as though with Christ, before God before men.

In the Spirit

'As we give ourselves to the Holy Spirit', a friend writes to me, 'our prayers may take various forms, from the words of psalms and hymns to a simple word like "Jesus", or to a pleading for particular people or situations which catch our imaginations or involve our various feelings.'—'Standing before God, the one who stands is himself before God, but also is the representative of everyone else and in particular of those who have made him what he is and who impinged on his life in any way.' So 'a particular person with either a particular need or a particular relationship to the one praying can become the centre of attention'. Then one can move through that to God so that one's being can become fixed on God, 'through the other, as though they were an ikon or a keyhole into reality. Moving back one may then see that person in a new way'.

These words at once recall another description of prayer which can enlarge our whole understanding of what it means to be a Christian, Arthur Wallis's *Pray in the Spirit*. For him also, prayer begins in the act of faith by which we surrender ourselves to be freely at the disposal of the Spirit. Jesus Christ himself, the wounded man at the heart of God, is the Witness, the Advocate who, by his very continued presence at the centre of all being, is a continuous prayer for us. When at the outset of prayer we are still and seek to yield ourselves, the Spirit who flows from Jesus becomes a witness and an advocate with us and through us, praying in us. We put our jumbled minds and hearts in his path, and he shapes out of our confused awareness his themes, brings before us a verse, a picture, an insight, a need, until we can say, in Kepler's words, 'O God, I am thinking your thoughts after you'. Even in our weakness the movement of our little broken consciousness can become his.

You can become aware then of a deep inarticulate yearning within which joy and sorrow fused, a kind of 'passion of the Holy Spirit', a prayer travail, which carries with it its own almost involuntary burden of pain. You can touch on the mystery which Charles Williams called 'coinherence' by which in prayer you may be enabled across time and space to enter into the sufferings of others, into the agony and longing of the universe itself. Wallis gives the evidence of those who have been plunged even into weeping, into a kind of groaning or sighing right within them, as well as sometimes breaking through beyond into that momentary glimpse of glory in which we, in Vaughan's words,

> feel through all this fleshly dress
> Bright shoots of everlastingness.

This almost physical sense of yearning may not be the experience of many. But all Christians are called to prayer at this depth. They can at least be enabled by the Spirit to make that small share of the world's frustration which is theirs, deep within them, into their part of Christ's prayer for the whole creation.

The man of prayer, like Staretz Silouan, must be given by the Spirit what he cannot arrive at, of himself, purity of heart. This purity is an integrity which draws together all the rich variety of human experience, of happiness and of grief, of wounds and of healing. It is an integrity which the great artist knows, as it were, by proxy. But the man or woman of prayer must know it in reality and can do so only at the Cross.

Alan Ecclestone in his *Yes to God* is wrestling all the way through with this holding together of all the world's fragments of awareness. Our preparation for prayer, in his view, must entail a real effort to inform our minds and hearts as to all that is happening. We may be helped by art and poetry. We must be conscious of political and social struggle, the cry of the oppressed. Our prayer must 'embrace the mighty and poor as did Christ's mother in the Magnificat'. We must be conscious too of the new ordeals of doubt and precariousness many are passing through, the loss of familiar certainties, the loneliness and strangeness of the new world now emerging, of which he remarks that men have to 'work out a way of living in it, very much as the first moon-walkers had to find ways of placing their feet'.

New pain has entered man's world. Passion must plumb new depths of stress and alienations. Prayer must reckon with the wilderness of urban industrial life in scenes remote from the leisured, cultured security in which so much earlier spirituality was set. Prayer must 'embrace and sing ...

almost as Teilhard de Chardin does in the *Mass of the World* every scrap of the chronicle of the experience of the Ascent of Man and see with equal seriousness the challenge to the meaning of life which Treblinka and Auschwitz posed'. Only the Spirit can give us such a far-reaching magnanimity, as to be 'burden bearers of creation' and arrive at a Benedicite, a song of worship, interleaved, like the *African Sanctus*, with a whole scrapbook of the discoveries, the despairs, the shocks, the surprisings, the exhilarations and the horrors of life in our present world.

The new wave
For I believe the Spirit is matching the changes in human existence with a profound change, a universal quickening in the life of the Body of Christ, the Church all over the world. That kind of New Testament prayer which has for centuries been preserved on Mount Athos is suddenly become multiplied in the context of new, richly corporate life. Contemplative prayer is no longer for the few. It is being *democratised*

> as we discover again the New Testament experience of the fulfilment of Joel's vision of the Spirit poured out on all flesh. In an unprecedented response to unprecedented change in the world we sense a new wave of that stream of personal charismatic life and awe which flowed with torrential might from Palestine on the Roman world in a new springtide of the Spirit.

We cannot, like some commentators, domesticate it within tradition, or neutralise it within sociological or psychological categories. It is a worldwide wave of prayer, 'a tidal wave of the coming kingdom' in Alan Ecclestone's words, here visible, here hidden. For house-groups or for isolated members of the body scattered far from the rest, a new Telstar-like consciousness is coming into being as we are caught up into an invisible network of adoration and intercession and become, with a new vividness, members one of another.

New calls to prayer in the Spirit must go out as we are drawn into this flow of praise and yearning. At such a moment as this in CMS we are seeking to develop in Selly Oak what began at Foxbury and to keep at the new Leasow House, our centre for missionaries and other members at Crowther Hall, a continuous stream of prayer right through the year daily at 10.30 to 10.50 in the morning, a coffee-break prayer time of intercession. We are hoping many of us everywhere can join in together, however briefly, even for a minute of quiet inner attention at coffee-time, bringing together groups and individuals from Cairo or Khartoum to Quetta or Kampala; from new cells forming in, say, a struggling congregation in Isfahan to the discovery of a new uprush of Christ-centred fellowships in Fiji, finding the Spirit 'touching their weaknesses in practical ways and renewing them' as everything—confession, intercession, caring for each other—'seems to flow from a deep praise' and a welcoming attitude to life in all its circumstances.

At the end of his book *Disciple* Juan Carlos Ortiz calls us to get into the waters of God's love until we cannot touch the bottom and are taken where the river wants us to go. Arthur Wallis, too, says we must be plunged into the river of the Spirit—'waters to swim in, new depths to be explored, new resources tapped, new power to be released, so many of the deep things of God are still to be discovered'. 'The world' he says, 'has yet to see such a manifestation of the glory of God as can only come through a Church cleansed and purified, praying in the power of the Spirit.'

The tide is moving. May we be carried far.

Recommended reading

Books:

Archimandrite Sophrony, *The Monk of Mount Athos*, (Mowbray, 1973).

Arthur Wallis, *Pray in the Spirit* (Victory Press, 1970).

Alan Ecclestone, *Yes to God* (Darton, Longman & Todd, 1975).

E. Kadloubovsky and G. E. H. Palmer, *Writings from the Philokalia on Prayer of the Heart* (Faber, 1951).

John Carden, *Morning, Noon and Night*, (CMS, 1976).
R. M. French, *The Way of a Pilgrim*, (SPCK, 4th edition, 1972).
Record:
David Fanshawe, *African Sanctus*, (Philips, 6558 001).

Prayer: A Double Rhythm

Again and again I find my thoughts returning to the theme of prayer—not surprisingly, since this above all is central to everything we are doing. I recall a Cameroonian pastor who, while studying in this country, visited an Anglican Community of Sisters near Oxford, which immediately reminded him of a monastic community in his own land. He tried to describe something of what this experience meant to him. 'I have come to the feeling that a new power of communication is about to replace the ageing concept of mission [institutions] . . . With groups and communities like these, nothing can replace the love of hearts, God's love in living action.' He spoke here of sensing a new movement, a hidden work, a transformation at the roots, as it were, that is going on despite the outward changes that have yet to be made in society.

Way of being
The 'way of being' is essentially the conviction that people *by what they are* can affect structures. This isn't the old pietism (change individuals and the structures will change themselves); rather it is the recognition that the real source of the spiritual power which in the end alone can change structures can begin to work even while it is embodied only in scattered individuals and small groups. The secret of this spiritual power, this quality of freedom and yet of passion, which can transform the universe, is prayer. Faith begins in mysticism and goes out in politics, as Péguy said. Genuine prayer in the Name of Jesus is the most profoundly potent transforming power.

Christian prayer is not, as many activists would think, a cultivation of oneself, some kind of hobby for the devout, practised individually. Christian prayer is participation in a central purpose, a sharing in a movement of love working through history. Indeed, the Eastern tradition sees it as a sharing in the transfiguration of the universe, in the transformation of creative being at its very heart. Prayer has become institutionalised and individualised, but true Christian prayer is fundamentally a moving of the Spirit of Jesus in the hearts and minds of men, preparing the whole creation for the final reconciliation, and working towards the gathering up of everything into Christ the Son. It is a movement which the Father is bringing about.

To pray in the Spirit through Christ to the Father is therefore not a private matter at all: it is, rather, to put ourselves as little tiny fragments of the plan into the will, into the way, into the stream which through all history—through every time and place and situation—is drawing on towards a final goal when everything will be gathered up and God will be all in all. As we begin to seek this kind of prayer, suddenly we experience ourselves as strands in a much vaster purpose, each one of us called to fulfil our own small part. We find ourselves homing in, drawn into a convergence on a central theme—a theme that was given in Jesus Christ crucified and risen.

Once we recognise this we cannot doubt the importance of creating a still centre, of making a kind of desert-place, a place of silence and stillness somewhere in our lives. We may find that a particular place, even a particular physical attitude, will help us to achieve this stillness. Caffarel has shown how even our bodily positions can provide a language beyond words: the way in which we place ourselves, in which we move, our very quiet breathing, perhaps the repetition of a word as we gradually draw into a Presence closer than breathing itself. At this point we get a sense of coming to One who loves and welcomes us. Nothing is more distinctive of Christian prayer, perhaps, than this sense of being expected, of having access. I think so much reluctance to pray arises from the thought of prayer as a forbidding duty and of God as somehow distant and severe. But the moment we achieve that stillness, we discover that the Presence into which we enter radiates a sympathy, a forgiveness, a love that wills to draw us, that longs for us to enter into his movement.

Such a sympathy and such a forgiveness are likely to produce tears. Indeed, it may be that we must be broken to reach this point, that we have to cry 'Lord, have mercy', but we come with a simple conviction and trust, as we dwell on a word or a verse of Scripture, maybe on the Name of Jesus himself. 'Bind the mind with the thought of One only,' said one of the ancient Fathers, 'hold no intermediate image between the mind and the Lord.' Or, as the *Cloud of Unknowing* has it:

If you want to gather all you desire into one simple word the mind can easily retain, choose a short word which the Spirit can bring to mind. Use it to beat up on that cloud of darkness above you, and to subdue all distractions, consigning them to the cloud of forgetting beneath you. Should some thoughts go on annoying you, demanding to know what you are doing, answer them with this one word alone. If your mind begins to intellectualise, remind yourself of the simplicity of this one word, and your thoughts will vanish.

We are, says the ancient tradition, to enter thus into a darkness, a nakedness, a littleness, penitent, humble, small.

And so we find that as we enter into this stillness and into this love and forgivingness we become more and more conscious of a deep assurance that God loves us, and more and more ready to share in his Son's great *I am*: I am because I am loved. We must open ourselves to be infilled, possessed, grasped by the love of the Spirit. Sometimes this happens best through a mutual ministry, a friend praying with us and laying hands upon us. Often it can happen simply on our own: we can sense the Spirit welling up within us. Other things will well up too—anger, darkness, hostility, bitterness, pain—and it is only as we continually repeat the phrase or the Name, continually seek to draw more deeply into the Presence, that we can discover how these can be accepted and integrated.

Certainly we need each other's help in this, and I think that the growth within small groups of a deep candour and trust, of honesty, of mutual listening and understanding and acceptance, is very important. But essentially where we are to find ourselves is being held in love, and it is as we are held in that love that processes of change become possible within ourselves. Here I am able to be just who I am, not a saint, nor a sage, nor a hero—just a forgiven sinner. Prayer becomes breathing itself—that is why some of the Fathers in the past wanted to adopt the Eastern method of making the Name of Jesus part of one's very breathing, not simply as a technique, but to symbolise the very fact that prayer is what we are, and that it is the Spirit of Jesus moving within us and integrating our inmost being.

Beat of two wings
As we are held in the dual tenderness and severity of this great love, as we are both judged and forgiven, searched and affirmed, we begin to be able to respond. We are ready for some kind of use, and we find that response moves in a twofold rhythm: thanksgiving and worship on the one hand—quiet, wordless love that has been called silent music, with bursts of joy and praise—and, on the other, a response of deep yearning and longing, and pain that so much of the world is absent from that light and joy.

The first, epitomised in those great thanksgivings of St Paul's prayers, takes us into that joy which ultimately enfolds all creation, that rejoices in God as when the morning stars sang together and all the sons of God shouted for joy. We begin to touch then on an ultimate inner gladness which marks the faces that I have seen all round the world of those who know and love God. Once we know ourselves to be freed and loved, the Spirit within us seems to be enabling us to hail Jesus as Lord, or to cry out *Abba! Father!* It is something of this joy in worship that is being recovered in so many parts of the world-wide Church through the charismatic renewal.

And yet this joy is so often drawn out of deep wells of suffering: the most joyful faces bear the refining marks of struggle and pain. Light blazes out of darkness, bursts of praise as in the Apocalypse cascade into being against the night. The final fulfilment is now and yet not now, not yet. The central focus of Christian contemplation is always on the wounded Man in the heavens. He ever lives to make intercession for us. The closer we are to this God in Christ, the more he plunges us back into the creation in which he is involved. At the centre of Jesus' teaching on prayer is the story of the importunate widow, where prayer is seen as a beating upon the very gates of heaven, until God shall vindicate his elect.

And here we move into the other half of our response, into an earnest, intense, concentrated intercession, a remembering of people and situations within the Presence, a discovering of them deep in the heart of the love of God in which we have become immersed. This remembering is an active, imaginative work: the Spirit within us broods upon the chaos, calls forth faces, places and situations, explores the very depths of the world around us, enables us, empowers us, to remember those that are in bonds as though we were bound with them, and to suffer with those who suffer adversity, being ourselves in the Body (Hebrews 13). Christians remember their fellow beings with every news bulletin, and are caught up in this intense and mysterious call to watch and pray. We learn what it is to depend on each other's prayers more than we can ever know.

This intercession is shown as being so essential to the whole activity of God in the Bible that I believe that it is here that the breakthrough is to come, here that we are being called to go deeper if we are to see the renewal of the Church and the changing of the world. Intercession is a form of compassion in action, an entering into God's heart of caring and into the very place where he bears the world's hurt. It is an act of love. It is a longing for others to experience what we—albeit weakly enough—experience ourselves. It is a profound seeking for the salvation, the wholeness, of all, for the making of all things new. Perhaps this is where we find the mystery of Jesus' specific instruction to pray for our enemies, those beyond our human sympathy and love, small as it is.

Here, once again, pain and yearning are never far from thanksgiving and affirming. Very soon we shall find ourselves giving thanks for those for whom we are praying. Indeed, there is a subtle sense in which intercession can, without that thanksgiving, be always making an implicit contrast between the needs of others and our own apparent adequacy. St Paul again and again thanked God for others —for their gifts and their insights, for his making them more fully themselves. As we follow his example, as we pray for each other in that context of thankfulness and affirmation, so we shall be given afresh to each other. Such intercession mingles praise and yearning as it breaks barriers, releases impositions, lifts burdens, transfigures lives, opens up, undergirds, supports, all that we do and are.

The one meeting point
How can we hold together these two aspects of prayer, the 'now' and the 'not yet'? How can we be kept in this incredible poise, this balance of grace, sensing the abyss of sorrow and yet the height of joy, holding together darkness and light, serenity and yet passionate involvement? Worship and yet agonised yearning, delight and yet a chastened sense of our wretchedness? How can we face reality in such a way as to be neither romantic and sentimental nor sceptical and disillusioned?

Such prayer is really seeking to do what great art does—to face the ambivalence of life with a kind of final hopefulness, not without irony, a tragic confidence to hold together the masks of the stage. The man of prayer in Christ must so engage with the depth of what is happening all around him that he never attempts to evade or to break beyond it, but seeks always to work *through* it. Grace has to be able to contain and to transcend the terrible incongruity and contradiction of life. And there is only one Person and place in all the world—beyond the world, too—where these have been contained and ultimately resolved. That Person and that place are Christ and his Cross. Only in the power of his resurrection and in the fellowship of his sufferings do we see the integration of these two opposed aspects of experience.

He is at once the Source of life and the Man of sorrows; only in him is released a love which bears all things, believes all things, hopes all things, endures all things, which holds darkness in light.

This is the point to which in the end all faiths and spiritualities are coming in this time of change. It is the point to which they must come if they are to be true to the whole of reality as it emerges more clearly in the travail through which they are all passing in this present time. Unwittingly, unknowingly as yet, they are being drawn nearer and nearer to the Cradle and the Cross, where praise and intercession mingle freely until the one passes into the other, where prayer that is true to the whole of life becomes entirely possible, and where men, beasts and all created things will find their true home at the last.

Recommended reading
H. Caffarel, *The Body at Prayer* (SPCK, 1978).
Igumen Chariton, *The Art of Prayer: an Orthodox Anthology* (Faber, 1966).
Kenneth Leech, *Soul Friend* (Sheldon Press, 1977).

Love Will Out

'What is the significance' asks Max Warren in *I Believe in the Great Commission* 'of the convergence of so many seekers on the Jesus of history? I believe that the simple answer is that Jesus offers a quality of salvation which, slowly but surely, men are coming to realise can be found nowhere else.' This theme of the convergence of all men on Christ sums up so much not only of the message of Max Warren's magnificent last book but of his whole life and ministry. Characteristically the book points us forward to the next phase, for always, like the prophet he was, Max went on ahead of us, reaching out into the unknown.

Some years ago I had a disturbing and exhilarating visitor. Ahmed, as I will call him, would be surprised to hear me describe him in this way. He is such a gentle friendly person. It's just that his own deep evangelistic concern somehow convicts me.

I had last seen him on the edge of the desert. We had walked together then under the stars, had sat and talked in the courtyard of his family home. I remembered every detail of his story, of the long passionate search which led him by way of the Muslim Brotherhood, Sufi mysticism, and many another turning. Then the Living God in Christ embraced him, met his fears and griefs, and filled his whole being with the realisation that he was loved and forgiven.

We took up the threads again. There he sat, so entirely himself, grizzled hair, with the tribal marks that had been cut on his cheeks in childhood and the sculpting that years of seeking had left on his still open face. He looked at me searchingly, quizzically, yet with characteristic tenderness, all unwittingly testing how far my concern survived the change in surroundings, the suburbs, the commuter line, the committees, the office. Were there veils of irrelevancy to be pierced by those keen eyes? Would he find the same priority we had felt that night as lorries rumbled across the desert towards unknown towns beyond the horizon and we dreamt of a new evangelistic movement?

Crucial theme
After all, he was a man possessed by love, quietly confident of the one thing needful. He travelled light inwardly, conscious night and day both of a divine burden and a divine ease. He could sit there smiling, and chatting, and tell folk stories to the children, and yet you knew he was a man with a quest. Someone with that urgent sense which discoverers and artists have of being on the edge of some great new integration. Someone moving easily through the foothills of a place of unprecedented spiritual opportunity.

Like so many an evangelist out of Africa and Asia he knew intuitively the truth which we have not yet reasoned our way to, we who have lost so much of the faith and fire within us. He knew that to become truly ourselves we all of us have sooner or later to be grasped by a Personal Love coming to us from beyond ourselves. This is to be the source for us of a new identity and a new shape to society.

In Ahmed this Love, reflected, carried conviction because it had about it both the simplicity and the complexity of reality. He had that aliveness to everyone and everything, that zest and curiosity, that relish for the incongruity of things which is the very spring of real humour and real faith. Such a life confesses, proclaims, the one Source of all compassion and all delight. This is what I must share with you, it seems to say, because I cannot contain it alone. Woe to me if I do not declare it with my whole being. It breaks out of me and cannot be repressed.

When I knew there was a God, I danced upon the Brig o'Dee!

And because this gift, this sheer grace, is truly personal it is never merely individual. Far from it. It is the very motive energy that will bring into being and multiply groups, communities, 'cells of dissent', of the kind which alone will serve to transform society. Little organic groups of the kind that might gather in Ahmed's courtyard, or in my sitting-room, and within which each member is cherished and confirmed in his own being. Each group at home and welcoming to anyone, without exception, but yet having its own intrinsic character, its roots in God in Christ, its essential theme.

Such groups could be scattered through the world like burning fragments, setting so many others ablaze. They could offer men the opportunity to experience alternative patterns not only of self but of the structure of society. Evangelism of this kind is not proselytisation with its overtones of calculation and pressurising. It is the spontaneous communication of a way of praying, a way of being. And it speaks in the one universal language of a genuinely humane, disinterested and humble love, which transcends all barriers, and attracts all creatures.

Crucial moment

The talk with Ahmed ranged out this time as last over a whole network of restless seekers within Islam and other ancient patterns of faith. A movement was stirring in the hearts of many, of those often younger than Ahmed, drifting into towns and wandering the streets of growing cities. In so many parts of the world the time is ripe for an up-rush of 'faith active in love'. The Gospel was first proclaimed and the Church first grew in the midst of a critical melting down of cultures and faiths, 'gods many and lords many', with a number of the same ingredients in the mix as today. Ahmed became a spokesman for countless pilgrims, one among the searchers, prophets, poets, leaders of cults and movements, who have been attempting intuitively to feel the way forward for whole societies in transition.

The more formal traditional kind of society in which

Ahmed grew up has been compared to a mesh or grid. The dividing lines are the rules which separate men from women, the wealthier from the poorer, the older from the younger. As you grow up all your relationships, your responses, many of your choices and decisions, are guided by these fixed externally imposed conventions. Once modern economic and political change comes the grid begins to slip, the rules begin to be broken, the roles confused, older people often feel as if the world is collapsing.

> Untune that string
> and hark what discord follows . . .

But many of the younger, especially the more perceptive and far-sighted, begin for the first time, instead of looking back to the tradition, as their forebears have done, to feel forward for some new shape of society, some new self-understanding which could serve better at such a juncture. And this can genuinely be a movement of opportunity offering at least the possibility of a rich full realisation of personal life.

In the nineteenth and twentieth centuries Africa, like so many other parts of the world, offers many examples of whole successions of spiritual movements, intuitively seeking for new patterns. The stories of such sequences underlie and peep through histories of the Church, such as the tremendously perceptive little history of the East African Church by W. B. Anderson. There were some of the 'prophets' such as Mwai wa Mwanguwa at Mbale in Kenya, Kighobo the prophet of Usambura in Tanganyika or the famous Kikuyu seer who figures at the beginning of Ngugi's great novel *The River Between.*

In West Africa there were a whole series of witchcraft cleansing cults, each with its special dances and songs and emblems, like similar movements in Central Africa, with the same kind of future expectation of new community and prosperity. In Zaïre, the ecstatic prophet of the Ngunzists figures with similar promises. The cargo cults of the Pacific, the intensified expectation in nineteenth-century Java of the coming of a messianic king, are variants of the same universal theme. So many societies have had and go on having their own diverse forms of forward aspiration with its new openness to the Personal.

Crucial form
It is into this kind of sequence that so often the Christian gospel comes. Missionaries, people from outside the culture, with their own forms of doctrinal and liturgical expression, can never be more than midwives, or, in a stricter analogy, implanters of a seed. The real process can never be a conscious borrowing, as in the case of the 'readers' as the first generation of young East African Christians were so often called. Anderson brings out the point that what was often called *kusoma* Christianity (kusoma=to read) and the literacy movement that went with it spread through the school—dispensary—church process. But Revival or, in Kenya, *roho* Christianity (roho=spirit), springs organically and spontaneously out of the sequence inaugurated by earlier prophets.

The whole story of Simon Kimbangu illustrates how this can happen. The epic of Kimbangu and his great Church in the Congo has been well told by Marie-Louise Martin. The conviction he embodied was the same assurance that God is with his suffering African people as they wrestle with colonialism leading them out into a new future. Kimbangu became a symbol that Christ is 'God with us'—not a pale remote figure from a world beyond, but a fellow sufferer.

The equally moving and astonishing story of the growth of the Church in East Java, as Philip van Akkeren tells it, shows that it was only indirectly the Dutch missionaries, mainly at the coast, who brought the Gospel which was to attract such astonishing numbers in the world of Islam and the traditional cult of the rice spirit. It was much more C. J. Coolen, half-Javanese, half-Dutch patriarch, in middle age leaving the colonial government service to withdraw inland to the old heart of Java and to start his own plantation and community. In a way entirely true to the elaborate rituals of dance and puppet play inherited from his mother, he taught and enacted his own version of the Gospel. Once again the message that dawns in their imagination and soul is that of God come near to us and with us. A feeling of *slamet*, of salvation, of:

> the reassuring knowledge that no-one in the community has anything against us, that no power above or below can dominate or hinder us, and that in Christ a social and cosmic peace will be achieved . . . peace of mind, a release from inner conflict and from feelings of guilt and the fear that sometime a law has been broken . . . experienced collectively in the Church or meeting rather than as individually as in Western pietism.

Crucial response

The coming of Christ in such a valid form will evoke its own appropriate response. It may be a response with significant implications for a society's needs and problems. In Zaïre the Kimbanguist Church, now three million strong, in spite of massive persecution and deportation has developed its own schools, agricultural projects, training programmes, even hospitals, without a touch of aid from outside. Many members are keen evangelists. They also support each other in their own little cell groups for prayer, mutual confession and help. The Church with its emphasis on non-violence and positive practical care has been described by a secular agnostic observer of the Zaïrean scene as 'the most constructive social reality in the country'.

In East Java the many prototype Christian rural communities which followed Coolen's and were led by his disciples made a vital contribution to the redevelopment of rural life and agriculture at a time of crisis.

Missionaries write from various parts of the world describing new apprehensions of the Gospel arising from within the heart of changing religions and culture, fresh visions of 'God with us' in person, in Jesus Christ. One friend is working alongside whole scattered groups in a Muslim society who for generations have been loyal to a quest for a new grasp on Jesus approached from within the Qur'an itself.

They make the point that the role of the agent from outside, the evangelist from a different race, class and culture, must be minimal. There, as here in the housing estate, the inner city, the shop floor, the forms of the gospel and the response to the gospel must arise intuitively and spontaneously from within. The seed grows secretly. Those nurturing it can only stay at the fringe trying to be patient and perceptive and offering their friendship, their readiness to be vulnerable.

The lessons of Roland Allen's *Spontaneous Expansion of the Church* still apply today. He pinpoints the way in which the well-meaning efforts of us clerics and professional Christians can so often still today smother vital sparks of new faith and life which could have set whole worlds ablaze. Organisation, training and the maintenance of standards can destroy the very growth they were intended to safeguard.

The evangelist's main task is to trust, to love and to connect where he can. It is the Christ lifted up in the patient and humble quiet of his heart who is most likely in ways beyond his knowing, to draw others. As to his priority there can be no doubt. He has no need to assert it further. If we can live and act in such a spirit, then I believe great prospects open up before Ahmed and ourselves working together and learning from each other and from those to whom we are sent.

Recommended reading
Max Warren, *I Believe in the Great Commission* (Hodder & Stoughton, 1976).
W. B. Anderson, *The Church in East Africa, 1840–1974* (Central Tanganyika Press, 1977, available in UK from SPCK).
Marie-Louise Martin, *Kimbangu: an African Prophet and his Church* (Blackwell, 1975).
Philip van Akkeren, *Sri and Christ—a Study of the Indigenous Church in East Java* (Lutterworth Press, 1970).
Roland Allen, *The Spontaneous Expansion of the Church* (World Dominion Press, 1960).

In Search of a Whole Gospel

The scene was the fringe of a South American city, one of those *favelas*, *bustees*, shanty towns which form the makeshift outskirts of more and more of the growing cities of the Third World. A Westerner was wandering through it, increasingly appalled by the all-too-familiar sights of such areas: the pinched faces of the children, most of them with little future save a life of long burning days and pitifully short years; the women, the mothers, with the young faces already ageing of 'those who hold up half the sky'; the men, whose weary and shrewd expressions showed their long acquaintance with struggle and disappointment.

The man stopped to speak to a group who were working on a dilapidated car. He discovered they were Pentecostal Christians, helping each other through sharing the little they had and their individual skills. They invited him in to one of the shacks to join in the Breaking of Bread. One of the workers donned a simple white robe and there, with children peeping in through the window, my friend was welcomed into the kingdom of Jesus in the midst with simple and joyful dignity and courtesy.

Here was the heart of that little group's caring and sharing: they knew more than any of us the secret of the gospel. Here before his amazed eyes, the Magnificat was being acted out. Here the humble and meek began to enter into their ultimate inheritance, the hungry were filled with good things. So it must have been in the little Church of the New Testament and the early centuries. And the rich were not necessarily to be sent empty away: they too could share in the joy of community and the hope of the Lord if they would submit to his judgment, step down from the ruthless exercise of power and become ready to share their riches.

This is the quality of the kingdom-community to which Jesus calls his followers. It is the pattern of living described in the Sermon on the Mount by St Matthew and its parallels in the Gospels of St Mark and St Luke. It is the outworking of the 'new commandment' recorded by St John. It is the shared life of Acts 2 and 4, which St Paul depicts in 2 Corinthians 8, to which he summons the Church in 1 and 2 Thessalonians and in 1 Timothy 6:17—19; to which others recall the Church (James 2, 1 John 3:14—18). It is the assembly of the poor in spirit, which may demand of those who would join it that they give up what they have (Luke 12:33) and which can be contrasted with the wealthy and oppressive betrayers of Israel, the establishment (Luke 6:21; James 5:1—6).

Deadlock at Melbourne
How different from this our world church often appears today. No longer does it shine with that joyous freedom that is unconfined by the weight of wealth or institution. It seems rather to be locked into the world's pattern. Any world assembly of the Church today brings home to us vivid reminders of this contrast. A division between rich and poor runs right through the world Church—a division that would have amazed that vulnerable little flock whom Jesus, departing, prayed for and committed to his Father.

At Melbourne, Australia, in May 1980 I attended a meeting of the World Council of Churches' Commission on World Mission and Evangelism. Gazing around the conference hall I was made sharply conscious of this contrast. Of the 600 faces about me the great majority came from areas in Africa, Asia and Latin America where hunger, pain and oppression have their roots in poverty. Near me were others from relatively wealthier countries which yet also suffer under oppressive regimes. There were Presbyterians from Korea and Taiwan, some of whose fellow-churchmen are in prison for their faithful witness, on behalf of ordinary people, for justice. Not far away was a young

Baptist pastor from El Salvador who had been a member of the same ecumenical Bible-study group as the murdered Archbishop Romero. As we talked, he revealed in a quiet, matter-of-fact way, that he might well be shot within the next year. Ahead of me was a veritable 'hatscape' of different Orthodox headgear. Some of the owners were constant reminders of Churches once powerful but now being refined by persecution and experiencing even in Russia the stirrings of spiritual renewal.

It was moving as all the voices soared up in the sung prayer 'Your kingdom come, O God', which was itself the theme of the conference. But soon we were to hear less harmonious voices. They reminded us that we were entering the angry eighties, and the division between the rich and the poor that runs through our whole world opened up between us there at Melbourne. They were voices we would often rather not hear, voices of fierce indignation, cries of pain, anger and frustration, voices that spoke for the poor.

Increasingly we found ourselves in the grip of a deadlock in which the more that westerners strove to respond, the more they seemed to be distracted from those whose voices addressed them so bitingly from a pit of desperation.

The keynote had been struck right from the outset in the biblical exposition given by Dr Ernst Käsemann, the theologian of the conference. He re-interpreted with an apocalyptic fervour the battle of God's kingdom against the powers of evil. He set our whole study of the kingdom within the conflict of heaven and hell, the struggle of the kingdom of Israel with idols, the resistance of the saints of the Most High with the great beasts that rose out of the sea (Daniel), and the kingdom proclaimed by Jesus as a resistance movement against the demonic powers. Here he was, as it were, remythologising, seeing the demons as world-wide repressive economic and political structures, as western manipulation, as multinational companies, as reactionary militarism.

He knew the evil of which he spoke: three years previously, to the very month and week, his own daughter who had been working among the poor in Argentina, had disappeared, later to be found murdered—it was presumed by the ruthless forces of oppression.

This was the language that set the tone for all that followed. The theme of the kingdom lent itself to a number of Latin-Americans who had come hotfoot from scenes of violent oppression and slaughter and danger. Simply to be there with us, some of them had laid their life and liberty on the line.

Gospel with a vengeance

As the anger seemed to mount in all the main sections, the topics shifted. The very subjects for at least three of the sections perhaps fuelled the fires: Good News to the poor, The kingdom of God and this world's struggles, The Crucified Christ engages human power. In all these we seemed almost to lose sight of the Good News in our preoccupation with the bad news to the rich and powerful; to lose sight of the kingdom as we became immersed in this world's struggles; to lose sight of the crucified Christ as we grappled all too humanly with human power. We were faced with a picture of a world possessed.

At the centre of the stage forceful voices hammered at us, like that of an Asian pastor from South Africa. 'For how long must the suffering people of the Third World speak to the people of the western world? Are you so blind, so deaf, that you cannot see, you cannot hear? What do you want us to do—kneel, grovel, weep? You cannot repent. It will involve too much for rich nations steeped in oppression and greed. Why do we go on talking with you?' Or the Latin-American voice: 'Now is the second act. The people have taken what initiative they could in the first. Now the Church must respond to cries for justice.'

'You cannot repent . . .' Sometimes it seemed like that. We felt ourselves locked into the false structure, the false relationship, between North and South, a structure as rigid as the Law. And the representatives of the Third World could become locked into it too. Guilt on the one side, bitterness on the other. The violent voices seemed almost to assume a kind of alternative power—an establishment in reverse, like that of the Zealots in the New Testament. A theology threatened to prevail which, like all pure apocalyptic, brought about a straightforward inversion of the present order. It could divide the world, as Marx did, into oppressors and oppressed, rejecting the rich, the white, the middle class, without remainder. A strong exegesis would take the Dives and Lazarus tale (Luke 16:19–31) at face value.

The Bible which we Westerners had read so comfortably all these years, spiritualising away the many passages about the poor, had been freshly expounded back to us in a fierce judgment upon us. The gospel launched on the rest of the world in the nineteenth century from the West had now, after two world wars and the end of colonialism, come back upon us—appropriately, in Australia—as a boomerang, in the form of a call to repentance.

At the same time, the whole setting of Jesus' teaching about wealth and poverty within the renewed life of his kingdom-community, the special nature of his invitation into a sharing, forgiven and forgiving fellowship, seemed inadequately developed. Biblical terms like 'goodness', 'salvation', 'repentance', and some themes (supremely the crucifixion and resurrection of Christ), seemed at times to be pressed into the service of a purely secular transformation. The end result could have been to leave us bound by a new endless demand, a new Law. Sometimes the only repentance that was being urged upon us seemed to mean throwing in our lot with revolution, to destroy all that we had made and to start all over again. There was no acknowledgment of the formidable complexity of the present economic scene, and little of a searching critique of a possible future communistic alternative. It was as if we could see more vividly than ever the chains of sin that bind us ever more tightly, locking us into a pattern we are powerless to break. I felt again that we were in danger of being left captive in our respective guilt and resentment.

Redistribution of pain
But there was a saving grace at work, another movement

flowing through the depths of the conference. There were among the leading figures those who would point us in a different direction. The section on the Church's witness to the kingdom attracted many of those with a gentler approach, especially the Orthodox and the evangelicals. Bishop John Taylor, in an eloquent and stirring paper, pointed to ways in which the Church could even now be shaped to express something of the Good News of the kingdom.

Again, Raymond Fung, the Hong Kong industrial evangelist, summoned us to stand with the poor not only in the struggle for justice, but in a new way of living in which, as he had proved in little groups, the poor would come to find fulfilment in Christ. His paper 'Good News for the Poor' reflected his deep concern that the masses of the poor should be reached by the gospel. It was one of the few conference documents that was a sheer appeal for mission and evangelism. He spoke simply and clearly as an evangelist with a passion that the Church should be enabled to invite into the way of Christ those who properly should have pride of place within it. He pleaded that throughout the whole Church we should open ourselves to feel the very pulse and heart-beat of the poor, and that their tears should burn our cheeks.

Little of this evangelistic concern was really taken up in the discussion, or in the response of his section as a whole. The Latin Americans obviously appreciated the challenge to the rich posed by Fung's work. It was not so clear that they felt equally concerned that, in due course, once the poor had begun to lift their heads, they too should hear the clear call to repentance and the offer of forgiveness in Christ. And this in spite of other voices that were raised in the same plea. Emilio Castro, the warm and passionately committed Secretary of the Commission, kept reminding us of the call to spread the gospel even as we opened ourselves to the pain of the poor.

Kosuke Koyama, the Japanese theologian with a mine of paradoxical phrases, reminded us of the power of the suffering Christ, who always moves out from the centre of life to its periphery. Jesus was born in an obscure stable, lived and worked among outcasts and ordinary people, and died outside the gate. Through this very downward and outward movement he transcends and eludes our questions and our categories. He eludes us when we most clearly claim to have hold of him: he passes through the midst. In Jesus, God moves from underneath, works through the 'underside of history' (though for Koyama this concept would have a meaning very different from that attached to it by liberation theologians).

And there were faces in the crowd, voices in the discussions, that all the time seemed to point to the opening of another possibility between us all. Takami, the gentle Japanese sage from a Christian collective farm, whose quiet smile immediately reminded me of all the discoveries about life together in Christ that he has made in his little community of workers among the poor from all over Asia. Bishop Markos from the Coptic Orthodox Church of Cairo, with the passionate plea to his Latin American brethren which only he, coming out of a long-persecuted Church, could make, that they should never in the frenzy of their struggle lose Jesus. Or Bishop Banumoba from Uganda, whose very presence was enough to remind me of the deep discovery that the East African Revival had made of forgiveness and reconciliation between black and white, tribe and tribe.

Significantly, a real sense of participation came in the Bible studies in groups that were detached from the main organisation of the conference, with no space allotted for reporting back and no apparent way of influencing the main findings. It was here that everyone seemed to feel that they had been heard and had found a real meeting with others. In these small groups we also quarrelled, hurt and rejected each other, argued furiously, even wept.

In one small group, a Filipino member described the patronising attempt of a white assistant in a charity office to thrust upon her a coat that was manifestly not right for her. As she spoke, she began to weep, and this stung me, sparking off in my mind a kind of flashback of all the times when I had been patronising to those of other races, bringing home to me all the ways in which such hurtful 'superiority' is built into our whole western culture. Tears sprang to my eyes in answer to hers.

At the end, in our group as (I believe) in others, came a final reconciliation which was genuine and deeply moving. The most intransigent melted a little and went to meet the others. There was a real humbling and mutual discovery that 'what we need in the Church is a redistribution of pain'. And a special moment for me came in the final period of worship when the Filipino woman met me and, taking my hand, said: 'You have helped me; I now feel differently about it all.'

At certain moments in our worship, too, the repeated refrain 'Jesus, remember me when you come into your kingdom' became almost a singing in tongues, and the noble Orthodox liturgy caught us all up. But still there was always as yet an uncertainty, a lack of unity, as if we were still locked in our different bonds, uncertain of how to be loosed.

Another deadlock
Quite unexpectedly, the answer for me came a month later, at the other main world conference of Christians that year, also with the avowed aim of evangelism. This was a consultation of evangelicals, a follow-up to the great Lausanne conference of six years previously, this one being held at Pattaya in Thailand. The theme for this was 'How shall they hear?', expressing a concern for those who have not been reached by the gospel, estimated at some two billion.

Here, in contrast with Melbourne, I found an interest in other cultures, a world divided not into rich and poor, oppressors and oppressed, but into people's groups, small communities within a common culture (though in fact these groups proved quite difficult to define). The whole conference divided into 'mini-consultations' on how to reach people in different categories—Muslims, Hindus, Buddhists, city-dwellers, etc. The aim was to work for a growing cluster of churches 'for every people' by the year 2,000. If there was no sense of structural oppression, and no Marxist resonance, there was yet another kind of sociological jargon, that of 'diffusion of innovation theory', almost a kind of consumer research.

And yet here too we did seem at first to be locked into a rich/poor deadlock, bound into that same wrong relationship in which the affluent find themselves involuntarily depriving the poor. This was symbolised in our very place of meeting, a large luxury seaside hotel. For this was itself a monument to that wrong relationship between East and West: it was here that GIs had come for leave during the Vietnam war, and thus turned it into a centre of pathetic prostitution for rich western tourists.

The dominant culture in the ballroom where we met in plenary sessions was powerfully North American. There was a resounding message from Billy Graham. The atmosphere was almost that of an old-style rally. The good old favourite hymns were sung; speakers boomed away about strategies for church growth and the evangelisation of those two billion people. In place of the Marxist overtones of Melbourne there was an almost capitalist ethos of consumer research and methods of promotion. We seemed blandly unaware of the chains that bound us.

Here again there was a danger that the organisers might be too dominant, and perhaps even less accessible. Committees met behind the scenes to plan the main statements. Though contributions could be sent in or made in person, there were no floor microphones to give scope for comment or wider debate, as there had been at Melbourne.

Some of the main speeches and early reports suggested a potential spiritualising of the message, a separation of the content of the gospel from its political and social context, a relegation of questions about structures or the relationship between rich and poor to other groups. 'They are of course important, but *our* task is evangelism'—as if the two could be split apart. This had been a danger latent even in the Lausanne Covenant, which had set the two side by side. At Melbourne the Church sometimes seemed to have nothing distinctive to bring to the world because it merged into the world's ways. At Pattaya the Church was in danger of bringing nothing to the world because it was separating itself from the world and yet for that very reason remaining bound to it. In both places we sang in our chains.

Further movement
Yet here also, in that strange tender faithfulness of God, another movement stirred the depths. It erupted in striking testimonies, like that of a Romanian who had so loved his interrogator that, when he was released at the end of six months, the man told him 'I shall miss you', or that of an Indonesian woman who had given herself wholly to a costly and dangerous ministry among prisoners, living on very little. It irrupted in protests like that of a black South African who declared suddenly to a shocked meeting that his fellows could see no one group, ecumenical or evangelical, which was truly living as a South African Church. It emerged in a protest movement launched by Africans and black Americans, and joined by Asians, Latin Americans and westerners, which drew up an appeal for the conference to take seriously political and social witness—an appeal that became a vital conference document, influencing the whole conclusion.

Above all it appeared in some of the little consultations directed to seeing how to communicate the gospel to particular groupings. The leadership of the conference showed great confidence in these small groups, leaving them to work out their own reports which were exposed to an excellent discussion in a series of admirably open and well-chaired sessions. The final product here might prove to come rather nearer to the real feeling of the ordinary participants than any of the more large-scale reports from Melbourne.

In the mini-consultation which I joined, on the subject of the urban poor, the group seemed to go further towards a distinctively Christian response than had been possible in the total spiritual diversity of the groups I had experienced in Melbourne. Unlike myself, most of the members of this group were at work in poor areas in different part of the world. They too were diverse, but they shared more of a common expectancy and experience of grace. In spite of severe clashes, a spiritual unity emerged which seemed to go further even than that of our Bible-study group at Melbourne. Insights were opened up which gave us not only a foretaste but also a shared understanding of a break-through that might snap the world's chains. The Cross of Christ is being lived in the Body of the little communities, cells and teams that are multiplying all over the world.

We saw Christ on his Cross and in his resurrection touching and healing the structures of the world, releasing the deadlock inside each person. But in the same movement of love we felt and knew that the atonement, that profound reconciliation being worked out in the community of Christ, can come as a healing and a release to the outer structures too.

It seemed to me increasingly that what we were wrestling with was the relating of an understanding of the Cross of Jesus Christ and of our experience of him at two levels, which had become wrongly separated in recent years.

First there was the personal and the personalistic way of speaking about grace and God's love and acceptance. A view of the healing of God within us, restoring parts of ourselves to each other, bringing about the beginnings of a real personal integration. This belongs to a theology associated with the names of Gabriel Marcel, of Tournier, of Buber himself and Macmurray, who were popular and fashionable in the 50s and early 60s. It drew its language from psychotherapy.

Then had come a shift to the structural, the social and the collective, which so much possessed the theological mind in the 70s. This had become related so much more *externally* to social injustice and inequality. But these two belong together. Separated, the inner life and the social life become distorted by the same divisions, locked into the same false relationships. As Jesus Christ comes into the world, his sovereign force of grace, his fundamental forgiveness and atonement, re-integrates both microcosm *and* macrocosm.

As he bears the sins of each, so he bears the sin of the whole, personal and public, individual and corporate: his healing touches the structures of both inner and social life at every point.

Only as we begin to live out this integrating grace in a total response to Christ can the Body of Christ begin to offer a whole gospel to the world. Only then can there come a healing of that guilt and that resentment which at Melbourne were left largely untouched. Here is the breakthrough beyond the Law, a personal and corporate experience.

It was not that those who had borne testimony to personal experience of Christ's healing and forgiveness had been failing to speak of anything real, simply that we had not seen it in sufficiently comprehensive terms, that we were missing the whole in failing to see the corporate implications. In Christ, rich and poor *can* be drawn into a new sharing and caring relationship which releases both. At Melbourne we had focused on the world's pain, though in places we had touched on the healing. At Pattaya, for some at least, the healing of Christ became apparent in its fulness. An integral gospel emerged, with healing for individuals and society. Where such a gospel is lived and proclaimed, Christ can begin to be seen as the Desire of the nations, the Source of a new shared life.

A number of us returned to our countries longing to see this worked out further and to take our small part in it, longing to see a renewal of the sharing Church working through such small groups as the one I referred to at the beginning of this Letter. Longing, too, with as great a yearning, for a genuinely international mission working through and with the Churches already planted in each continent. Together we could begin to communicate a gospel that would bring a transformation not only to individuals but also to the societies within which each is set.

How shall we hear?
But the strongest 'how shall they hear?' or 'how can they be reached?' seems still to apply to the West. This is where the

boomerang returns. We need to see a movement like the campaign against the slave-trade, in which Christians with a strong personal and social Gospel commit themselves to changing our whole relationship with poor nations.

We need local renewal and an evangelistic movement in congregations; we need new mission areas in the countryside and in the inner city. We need a new mission from the Third World to the West which will help us towards a reorientation, both in the life of our Church and in our whole relationship with the rest of the world. But alongside them we also need to see the rise of a movement with the imagination and public will for change—a movement for which Edward Heath called in his courageous espousal of the remedies set out in the report of the Brandt Commission.

From these two gatherings, 'Melbourne' and 'Pattaya', we were summoned to respond with all our heart, hope and confidence to Christ's invitation to join his kingdom-community. Those of us who are relatively rich in this world's benefits must submit our life, individual and corporate, to his searching judgment. Then will we be set free to become rich in 'good actions', ready to give and to share in a new dimension. Then, with all Christ's people everywhere, we will begin to lay hold on that real life which even now bursts through the false structures and strictures within ourselves and our society. Only thus can we be welcomed into the little churches of the poor as simply and joyfully as my friend in the South American *favela*. Only thus can our several bonds be broken in the great fulfilment of love that lies beyond us.

Recommended reading

Books

Lesslie Newbigin, *Your Kingdom Come* (John Paul Press, 1970).
Lesslie Newbigin, *The Open Secret* (SPCK, 1978, a fuller treatment of similar themes).
Andrew Kirk, *Theology Encounters Revolution* (Inter-Varsity Press, 1980).

David J. Bosch, *Witness to the World* (Marshall, Morgan & Scott, 1980).

David L. Mealand, *Poverty and Expectation in the Gospel* (SPCK, 1980).

Paul Harrison, *Inside the Third World: an Anatomy of Poverty* (Penguin Books, 1979).

North/South: a Programme for Survival, Report of the Brandt Commission (Pan Books, 1980).

Grace and Truth

Recently I met a girl who in a quite unexpected way found even more than she was looking for in a Buddhist monastery. She had gone there, like so many others, in search of truth and meaning. She had got some little way through her training when, browsing in the library one day, she came across a book called *The Way of a Pilgrim*.

The book is set in Russia and describes how the author, having heard in church St Paul's injunction to the Thessalonians to 'pray without ceasing', was deeply touched by the words and set off in search of someone who could explain to him how to respond to them. Eventually he found a holy man in the forest who taught him the Jesus Prayer. He was to say over and over again the words 'Lord Jesus Christ, have mercy on me, a sinner'. He would start by saying them aloud, relating them in his mind to the presence of God in Christ through the Spirit, and pausing after each repetition, then gradually the prayer would begin to become part of his mind, so that he could just think the words. Sooner or later (and for him it happened soon as he walked the quiet roads) he would begin to feel the words. They would become a part of his very being, descending, as the old Fathers put it, 'from the mind to the heart'. The prayer would begin to pray itself through you *with your mind in your heart*.

The girl was moved by the book and herself embarked on this prayer 'in the name'. It had an amazing effect. Increasingly she found herself focused, through the words, more and more on an unknown person and presence. It seems almost as if for her, as in ancient times, the name had conveyed the nature and the reality of the one to whom it belonged. The monastery seemed to burst open, the whole of her search to open up and, after only a fortnight, she was led, almost driven out, into a fresh struggle of a new kind, bringing with it confusion and pain but also a hidden excitement and hope.

Gradually, as she found her place in the right Christian community, the different parts of herself and of her life began to come together painfully, like a dislocation being put back. She was in the grasp of a gentle inexorable love, drawn into relationship with that central, crucified and yet risen figure. Here in his strange yet seemingly familiar love, she recognised the fusion at infinite cost, of a mercy and of a truth, tender and yet ruthlessly true to her, in which heavenly and earthly, spiritual and material, inner and outer life were being brought together. She was no longer escaping into some kind of tranquillity beyond. Here there was no evasion of any part of herself or of life. The Eternal God was with her and for her in the immediate demands here and now.

Holiness and wholeness
This girl had begun to experience a reintegration which we all need. It is really the heart of the renewal which the Church both desperately needs and is also eagerly discovering all over the world. It is a fresh realisation of the very gospel and message for which everyone is half consciously searching.

At the outset she had become aware, as have so many of us Westerners, that there is something we need from the East, something we can learn from the wisdom of the East, symbolised perhaps by her entry into the monastery. What she could not then know, as many of us still do not properly understand, is that the Christian Church has already, long ago, wrestled with that ancient Eastern contemplative philosophy. Israel was already in touch with Hellenism, through which Indian spirituality and thought were transmitted to the West, before Jesus the Christ was born. The wise men at his cradle could symbolise that fact,

Persian though they may have been. The New Testament Church preached and prayed in an already Hellenised world. The Early Church and the Eastern Church, from which the Russian Church sprang, lived and worked out their faith in Christ wrestling with that very Platonism in which major Asian themes found powerful expression.

Within this mystical environment the very quest for holiness itself, which many people in the West have recently embarked on, seemed natural. For the first thousand years of the Church's life, theology and prayerful contemplation were not separated. Christian theologians wrote out of their experience of God. They drew from the East, as from their Jewish forebears in the faith, that inner orientation of stillness, of rhythms of prayer, of spiritual direction for which Westerners now look to Indian gurus, Zen masters in Japan, Muslim Sufis (themselves Eastern influenced) or even the Jewish mystics of East European Jewry of the eighteenth and nineteenth centuries, the Hasidim.

We could perhaps equally well look to the earlier Church's Syrian roots—nearer to ecstatic possession and to the pentecostalism of the Montanists. This would bring us more in touch with African spirit possession and with that whole desperate longing for the Spirit to fall which characterises similar religious worlds. But what most writers about prayer fail to account for adequately is what happens when all this energy and longing become focused directly and fully upon the Person of Jesus Christ. What happens when, into this confused milieu of seeking and searching and struggling for fulfilment for ourselves, for others, for our world, *he* is born, bringing with him the only true wholeness?

The meeting place
Archimandrite Sophrony, Russian founder of an Orthodox monastery in Britain, author of an account of the life of Staretz (spiritual guide) Silhouan, a monk of Mount Athos, has described his own home-coming to Christ in *His Life is Mine*. At first, when he was an art student in Moscow, Eastern mysticism 'seemed to him more profound than

Christianity, the concept of a supra-personal Absolute more convincing than that of a Personal God. The Eastern mystics' notion of (ultimate) Being imparted overwhelming majesty to the transcendental'. It was only when he remembered Christ's injunction to love God 'with all thy *heart* and all thy mind', that actual knowledge appeared suddenly to him as a way of love. Then Jesus disclosed himself as the true love, sent from the Father, seen in the Spirit, not only transcendent, absolute, abstract, but present, personal and living; 'Being' eternally and yet immediately embodied, the 'I am . . .' So he shines out in a tremendous icon above the door in the hall of the monastery, portrayed on the cover of Sophrony's book, Christ enthroned, alpha and omega.

Here strange things happen as he dawns on all our broken worlds. All the enlightenment and wisdom of the sages, all the ecstasies and possessions of the mediums and prophets are not enough. Suddenly we realise, as the Christian fathers did, our true creatureliness. We recognise the great gulf separating us, even at our loftiest as at our lowest moments, from the living God. Our spiritual being is as far from him as our material being. Indeed, it is in our very brokenness and weakness, in our very recognition of our incompleteness, that he comes. He dawns upon us in our deepest night. Then most of all.

Prayer through Jesus is not just one way among a myriad others of varied types, faiths and lives. It opens up at the very least the possibility of a completely new realisation of God with us, and thus of our being able fully, wholly, with mind and heart, to participate in him.

There is an unparallelled realism in this Love. St John describes it in words that both recall and transcend (Exodus 34:6—7) as 'Full of grace and truth'. 'Rightousness and Peace are met together . . .' (Psalm 85:10). Most of our new Christologies in these days are too simple and sensible and rational to begin to comprehend the mystery. We have always tended either to separate Jesus from this world into a wholly ethereal docetic ghost, or to naturalise him totally into a wholly ordinary, mildly radical human. At Chalcedon they may have used alien and seemingly anachronistic categories, but at least their symbol was faithful to the essential insight of liturgy and sacrament and prayer in 'the name', of two opposite aspects held together in one movement of Divine Love, embodied and broken. In Jesus, contemplation in the Spirit encounters and is drawn into a meeting place of God and man, divine and human, eternal fulfilment and earthly tragedy through pain and death and resurrection. Then by faith we ourselves can be drawn through all our varied apprehensions of East and West, Asia and Africa, into the one great transfiguration of all things.

The way through

This transfiguration is an extraordinary mingling of suffering and joy, as you can see in the faces of the saints. On my journeys round the world, or even round Britain for that matter or even in my own office or in the CMS chapel at the Communion, I never cease to be surprised by those startling moments of recognition of what I often call a 'family likeness'. For me it explains the unity in diversity of the New Testament or of the whole history and life of the Church. In each differing culture and setting, every detail has changed, the whole pattern of life is quite unlike another, and yet there, like a tune transposed into another key, is the same immediately familiar 'relatio', the interrelation of heaven and earth, divine and human, the authentic reflection of the glory of God in Christ, in a human face,

Christ in ten thousand places
To the Father through the features of men's faces . . . !

Asian and African, meditative quest or drums, prayer in stillness or dancing and incantation are drawn alike into his dying and rising, pain and glory fused, to be 'oned' with God in him or possessed wholly by his Spirit. These many different witnesses are all describing an amazingly similar process of growth into Christ today.

As always, the key people tend to be those undergoing actual persecution or imprisonment. For them, the sharing in his dying is more obvious and clear. But all of us are called with them to a similar dying. In our age, when so many of the old frameworks of faith are falling apart for good as well as ill, and news of cruelty and horror spreads more swiftly, there must be a strong emphasis on enduring through the darkness and the numbness.

For many disciples discovering Jesus, the joy of the first apprehension of grace may not last long. There is usually a first vision of grace; there may even be a marvellous sense of mind and heart, soul and body, coming together and of new sharing with others. But this can be short lived. As the prayer of the heart opens out as we begin to be drawn further into Christ daily, we shall find that in him we also can only be made a meeting place for the Divine Spirit and earthly pressure at cost. To participate in this trans-figuration of the world round us we must expect to be drawn not only into meeting the needs of others, personal ministry, social or political action, but also into a much profounder intercession. Here again the Orthodox have much to teach us. As they prayed the Jesus Prayer often they have felt the weight of the sorrow and frustration of the world's groaning allied with their own inner groaning, as in Romans 8. Staretz Silhouan, the Mount Athos monk praying in the 1930s and 40s, was so poignantly oppressed by his own sin mingled with that of humankind that he cried out asking why, and God answered him in his heart with the mysterious words 'Keep thy mind in hell and despair not . . .' from which moment he was given a release. As we become such a meeting place there is a new hope also. Michael Bourdeaux has a great deal of rich inspiration for Christians round the world through his marvellous account of Russian Christians today *Risen Indeed*. He has described there some of the great prayer moments of our time. Anatoli Levitin, a prisoner in an isolation cell, walks round it repeating the words of the Orthodox Liturgy, praying the Great Litany for leaders and people in the Church:

'At the central point in the Liturgy . . . I felt myself

standing before the face of the Lord, sensing almost physically his wounded bleeding body. I would begin praying in my own words, remembering all those near to me, those in prison and those who were free, those still alive and those who had died. More and more names welled up from my memory . . . The prison walls moved apart and the whole universe became my residence, visible and invisible, the universe for which that wounded, pierced body offered itself as a sacrifice . . . After this I experienced an exaltation of spirit all day—I felt purified within. Not only my own prayer helped me but even more the prayer of many other faithful Christians. I felt it continually, working from a distance, lifting me up as though on wings, giving me living water and the bread of life, peace of soul, rest and love.'

Through our very weakness, failure and sadness, our emptiness, the Spirit flows, the light breaks. We will learn to live solely from grace, until 'grace upon grace' surprises us.

I found one of our workers in a village in Asia rising just before dawn to wait in the stillness and in the evening again poised in that quiet presence of Christ flooding us where we sat together with the forgiveness of God in the Spirit. This presence pervaded the friendships formed, the talks with the villagers, community work, irrigation, installing pumps, prayer with the sick, learning from the village Headman's wisdom. Individuals and groups all over the world are linked together yearning, rejoicing, interceding, beholding receptively; dying to self a little, being raised a little; waiting seemingly in vain or being touched by a miracle; darkened and yet light: through prayer in the name of Jesus, through the Word made flesh, drawn in one all-enfolding love. To him they will bring the sorrows and sighing of multitudes of the oppressed, to be turned into joy at last, the treasures of nations and cultures to be transformed and fulfilled.

Recommended reading
Donald Nicholl, *Holiness* (Darton Longman and Todd, 1982).
Michael Bordeaux, *Risen Indeed* (Darton Longman and Todd, 1983, St Vladimir's Seminary Press)

Archimandrite Sophrony, *His Life is Mine* (Mowbrays, 1979).
Andrew Louth, *The Origins of the Christian Mystical Tradition* (Oxford University Press, 1983).

A New Belonging

How many insights into the human condition have been arrived at in a tram or on a bus—in strange counterpoint to the impersonal and transient setting! In his famous study of Indian religion *Homo hierarchicus*, Louis Dumont tells the story of a young student in Paris, returning on a tram from a seminar with the great anthropologist Mauss. Suddenly he realised that he was looking at the people around him with different eyes. He saw every one of them as part of himself. He was no longer separate: all had their places in the whole.

Within the same era Péguy, stumbling between the seats of a similar Paris tram, in tears, saw the irreparable spiritual loss of his people. In Glasgow Edwin Muir felt himself and his fellow-passengers to be a collection of animals far from the immortality that was to become his quest.

Beyond individualism
The young anthropology student's 'secular' vision brought him strangely close to both Péguy and Muir, even while there was little in the Church or in theology to confirm him in it. For most of us in the West—including Christians—our picture of ourselves is much like the earlier view of that student. From the window of our swaying tram or bus we see blocks of flats or the suburban boxes in which we have walled ourselves off from each other or the tower blocks which have become their logical extension for inner-city dwellers.

The contractual view of society as a collection of

individuals loosely associated dates back a long way, even to the end of the seventeenth century. The industrial revolution accelerated the process. Our world emerged as a mass of isolated figures marked by that essential loneliness which permeates our art and our literature. The brashly triumphant urban and industrialised world spread over Europe and beyond it, everywhere selecting winners from losers, the successful few from the great mass of the 'also ran'.

It was essentially this individualism, dissolving traditional bonds of community, which missionaries took with them into the rich garden beyond Europe. Liberal Protestants and Evangelicals alike proclaimed a faith for the individual, helping to draw the newly baptised into a separate élite. Even the Tractarian and Roman Catholic emphasis on the Church made little difference: the Church itself was a sacramental institution through which individuals could wend their separate ways, like pilgrims lighting candles at differing shrines among the pillars of a gothic cathedral. Between them all, they spread the split that Europe already knew between social and 'personal', public and private, secular and religious. They nurtured a non-political, quietist faith with emphasis on individual virtues which easily conformed with colonial government and as easily, in many cases, yielded—even unwittingly contributed—to the tyrannies of the left or the right which so often followed.

Living in Berlin in the 1950s, I found that in its two worlds of capitalism and communism one half was at moments uncomfortably like a mirror-image of the other. For all my intense gratitude for the vital liberties of the West, the latter has a number of the same gaps and distortions as its rival. Strangely, in that divided city you kept encountering a haunting similarity between the two. There is in both the same sense of the 'lonely crowd', whether you are ruthlessly directed from above or as ruthlessly neglected by your fellows. Yet it was in that same city that I first stumbled on the seeds of a 'third way', in a revelation not unlike that of Dumont's student. I met a group of people whose whole attitude to life and relationships offered the beginnings of a different kind of society. A door seemed to open into the possibility of a world beyond both capitalist individualism and Marxist collectivism—a world which modifies and fulfils both, a world 'with a human face'.

Here was a pattern in which everyone had something to contribute, something to receive, everyone counted. There was a mutual openness and honesty. Barriers were lifted: people were free to acknowledge what they had been and what they wanted to be. And there was an openness to the world around—I had no sense of being in a closed club. The mutuality, the give and take, were to be extended and multiplied, demonstrated as the clue to what life was about.

The exchange
It took time to discover the heart and rock of this mutuality. The sense of a shared forgiveness, of an encouragement and affirmation of each other, a recognition of each person's special gift, had their springs in a central experience of mutuality: a mutual involvement of the divine and the human, God and man. Jesus Christ was seen as the *mitmensch*, God with us and for us, the one in whom God had involved himself in our loneliness and separation, facing the enmity and guilt which cut us off from him and from each other.

In that great image of the Fathers, God in Jesus Christ enacted an 'exchange' whereby as he enters into our life and death we are *together* enabled to enter into his death—and life. We participate in his self-giving, his cross-bearing, and are enabled to share his risen life. Christ himself has grasped us and is grasped as a corporate reality. The very figure whose words and acts were recorded in the Gospels becomes identical with the One whom we know as the theme, the rhythm and the motive influence of our common life. For those who recognise this and are willing to share in it, there is a new belonging, in which we begin to enter not only into each other's lives, not only into the shared life of Christ, but 'in him' and 'with him' into the very life of God: 'Our life is hid with Christ in God.'

This, then, is the beginning, the first 'sign' among us, of the kingdom of God—a life lived towards him and towards each other in 'the will'. And as that life starts to stir in us, so even through us healing, freedom and peace could begin to come in the midst of the world. The lonely crowds that are being bred by the modern great cities and the competitiveness of the 'rat-race' today are forced, in their struggle to survive, towards one extremity of living or another. Suppose that, wherever this new life of the gospel spread, they were stopped in their tracks by the goodness of another possibility altogether. Suppose they were enabled to glimpse the possiblity of a new kind of co-operation, a new quality of shared life. And suppose they were to see in that life the hope of a way of sharing not only with each other but with God himself!

Gospel of a new belonging

This must surely be the description of the real content of that elusive notion 'the renewal of the Church'. It is significant that charismatic renewal has carried with it from the outset a further potential (which also characterises allied developments in congregations which would not call themselves charismatic). That potential is the discovery of the meaning of 'the Body'. The significance of charismatic gifts has not been simply their character but their distribution. The very New Testament passages in which the gifts are described are discussions of the Church's corporate life: the Church as the Body of Christ. It is caught up into the life of God in what could be called a 'Trinitarian revival'. And it is from this emphasis on the Body that there necessarily flows a new recognition of the ministry of every believer, and a questioning of present patterns of 'ministry' and ministerial training, of worship and congregational life.

As such a renewal of the Church's corporate life takes place the Church becomes more what it was intended to be—the spearhead of the kingdom, the messianic community, the place where the disciples joined in the self-giving movement of love of their Master. This is the great insight of recent Mennonite writing in the work of men like Norman Kraus and Richard Mouw. For them the Church is the essential expression of the gospel. It is not seen as the kind of separate utopian group which once characterised little covenanting communities on the radical wing of the Reformation. Rather it is meant to be 'the incorporation of a new order in the midst of the old', marked by the principle of *koinonia*, participation, sharing in the self-giving of Christ. Here is the very opposite of both individualism and collectivism. The essential differences and the essential unity between each one of us are restored and we perceive our true 'coinherence', as Charles Williams called it. We are knit together in mutual intercession and shared praise.

Such a shared life immediately runs counter to the values of society all round it. In the eyes of 'the world' it must be a puzzle, a very evident practical 'secular' reality which is also a mystery. It must manifest the very quality of the life depicted in the Sermon on the Mount, imparted by Jesus to the first disciples and by the Spirit of Jesus through some of them, and through Paul, to the first little communities.

Not long ago, a town planner who developed a new depth of involvement on the part of ordinary householders with surprising success told me he was inspired by his experience in the Society of Friends. Think what it would mean if people with similar organisational responsibilities were constrained to initiate such change because of their vivid experience of the Church as the Body of Christ! The witness to their faith would be the way in which they affected the whole system in which they worked.

In other parts of the world also there is a genuine leaven of renewal at work. A little periodical launched in the 70s called *Full life—learning from one another* (CMS) was full of stories of ordinary congregations and small groups of Christians discovering the hidden resources locked up in their own fellowship. Through their activities, whether it be starting a new kind of shop, growing new crops or planting trees, changing health patterns, launching a local polytechnic to train the unemployed, they are stirring their neighbours to the same discovery. And the key to all such venture is the same—a transformation of the whole pattern of relationships. Indeed, development workers are seeing increasingly that in every sphere the real measure of 'development' must at heart be the degree of change in the amount of really strong mutual care.

For all such change one longs to see the Church becoming in modest, minor, broken ways something of a paradigm, a model, a showpiece of what grace can bring about—a fellowship of the *unlike* able 'to speak to the world of the possibility of genuine reconciliation and justice' because its members have begun to realise in their own life together the radical implications of God's reconciliation and because the effects of that reconciliation are all the time spreading outwards and touching others. Life in Christ cannot mean anything less than this.

The Gospel we have proclaimed these past 200 years has often been sadly individualised, privatised and spiritualised, or else reduced to mere moralism. However many hundreds of thousands across the world are converted, we must always ask: just what are they being drawn into? Too often it is to a fragmented experience or awareness of the gospel which has not stopped them from being in certain major aspects separated, individualised and conformed to their political and social environment.

There is an uneasy sense of this among many new Christians, an instantaneous recognition that something vital is lacking. Thus John Ray can write of a little group of new Kashmiri Christians:

The steady growth of this little band is most remarkable. Nearly all the converts have lost their jobs, nearly all are facing difficulties at home. Yet they stand firm, and that in our none-too-welcoming church ... T. has initiated an *anjuman* or association, a 'body' to welcome and bind together the recent Christians and new ones as they come in. Though a branch of it is, we hope, to be a Christian workers' co-operative, this is not its primary aim. Those who have become believers in Jesus feel very exposed as individuals, and so form 'a body'. It reflects the fact that our church . . . is *not* at present the body they are really seeking. A reading of the New Testament makes us sure that their instinct is a true one and that it is our (and your?) fellowship which has departed from the pattern and needs to return to it.

And must not this become a world-wide, transcultural, transnational, reality too, through a mutual interchange of people and resources, insights and skills and gifts? Isn't this what a society like CMS is really about—this universal renewal of the Body's essential life? A young Christian in a vitally growing church in an English town wrote to me while I was framing this *Newsletter*:

It seems that the Body of Christ has been disjointed, but soon the world will see the true power and majesty of God as the Church begins to function as it should, its members helping each other and really sharing together. We are beginning to learn more and more the need for real sharing even in our groups here.

They too are beginning to become what they are, part of the mystery of a new community of love in the midst of individualism and rivalry, part of the yielding up of self-seeking and the participation in the whole ongoing movement of God's love in Christ for which the world is still waiting.

Recommended reading

C. F. D. Moule, *The Phenomenon of the New Testament* (SCM Press, 1967).
Richard J. Mouw, *Political Evangelism* (Eerdmans, Michigan, 1973).

C. Norman Kraus, *The Community of the Spirit* (Eerdmans, Michigan, 1973).
Tim Lind, *Biblical Obedience and Development* (Development Monograph Series, Mennonite Central Committee, 1978).

Fearful Symmetry

I saw those wretched people streaming along the roads, poor miserable souls, carrying their bundles, all sorts of bundles. They were soldiers, each with a little pack on his back, barefoot, some of them already with sores on their feet which they bound up with rags ... I began to think about the Jews wandering through Europe and other places. One immediately rejects this idea. God in heaven, how can you compare the two things! Deep inside of you, you still have the feeling that it isn't quite like the wanderings and sufferings of the Jews.

Thus an Israeli soldier describes his reactions as he watched Palestinian prisoners marching by after the Six-Day War. This sudden uncanny flash of insight showed him his Palestinian victim as his own double. He very nearly accepts the thought. Kenneth Cragg gives us this excerpt (from *The Seventh Day*, Penguin 1975) in his own masterly study of the whole Arab/Israeli struggle, *This Year in Jerusalem*. This theme, of the mirroring of Jewish experience in that of Palestinian Arabs, leaps out at one from the whole story. The same thought has sometimes flashed out from newspapers and from television screens since the Israeli invasion of Lebanon. The Palestinian comes increasingly to be seen as the wandering homeless Jew of our time.

Both the Israeli Jew and the Palestinian Arab claim that one small strip of land by the Mediterranean as their historic homeland. Both are among the outstanding victims of injustice in this century. To right the wrongs of the one, the other was wronged in turn.

Twin yearnings
As Kenneth Cragg points out, the national aspirations of both these peoples were fed from the same nineteenth-century springs. The same kind of romantic nationalism, with its fervent dreams and rhetoric, which fired the imagination of Italians and Germans, gave rise to both a Jewish and an Arab literary movement. For the one it meant a revival of Hebrew, for the other of Arabic, the latter being fostered by Christian Arab writers and publishers. Meanwhile Islamic propagandists, such as Jamal al-Din al-Afghani, inspired the same kind of hopes in many Arabs as did the first widely read propagandist of Zionism, Theodor Herzl.

Arabs were then in occupation of what seemed one of the poorer parts of the Ottoman Empire, Palestine, where indeed they had been for thirteen hundred years. They could trace their indirect origins back nearly three thousand years to the Philistines and the later 'people of the Land' of the biblical story. They had been the main inhabitants for at least as long as the time of Jewish rule. Yearnings for national independence were already stirring among them. Their hopes were to be greatly strengthened by the promises made to them by the British and French Governments during the 1914–18 War. They naturally kindled to talk of 'the inherent right of self-determination of all peoples' and the like. Their aspirations began to find expression through a few spokesmen for what was largely a poor patriarchal society of subsistence farmers.

It was during the same period that Zionism began to find its first international apologists. They became spokesmen for the first modern generations of Jewish settlers in Palestine. These people, breaking beyond the tiny quiet remnant of orthodox Jews who already lived in the area, had embarked on a new venture. They cultivated the soil on their newly bought Palestinian land with an almost mystical fervour—as though they would redeem all the squalor and indignity of the long years of oppression. They envisaged a new redemptive community rising out of their labours. They were fired by a utopian liberalism and socialism, a heady idealism. It was not long before such motivation, empowered by Western-style resources and methods, began to give substance to their claim to 'make the desert blossom', as though Arab habitation and cultivation had never existed. This was propaganda likely to appeal to a Europe with colonial assumptions, let alone with a very bad conscience about its treatment of the Jews.

The appalling Russian pogroms drove larger numbers of Jews to find refuge in the expanding settlements. By 1914 the numbers had grown startlingly. And, as the settlers set up their stockades, their movement found in Chaim Weizmann a persuasive international voice. His subtle suggestions of some kind of possible aid to the Allied war effort, combined with his eloquent exposition of the Zionist case, met in Balfour, the British Prime Minister, with a blend of self-interest and genuine sympathy. Thus was secured the famous Balfour Declaration, with its promise of a 'National Home' in Palestine for the Jews. 'When I held the Balfour Declaration in my hand I felt as if a sun ray had struck me: and I thought I heard the steps of the Messiah.' It seemed the fulfilment of longing nurtured in suffering centuries long.

Significantly, in the Declaration the existing inhabitants of the land promised, the Palestinians, were never mentioned by name, even though the safeguarding of their rights was referred to. The world seemed to take its cue from the Zionists and to ignore the Palestinians from the start. Balfour himself, in subsequent correspondence brushed aside their claims in comparison with those of the Jews. Most Zionist reports, in spite of some eloquent Jewish protest, depicted Palestine as 'a land without a people sought by a people without a land'. Ben Gurion, forceful leader of the next generation, was to speak of 'a country without inhabitants in a moral and historic sense'. Meanwhile the million or so Arab inhabitants, disturbed by the large influx of newcomers and by the inroads of their strange culture, were already fearful. They knew nothing of far-away Jewish sufferings caused elsewhere by others. They could hardly appreciate the aspirations of the intruders. Over the previous millennium, they had shaped the countryside, the buildings and the culture. Their society had always made room, within its largely Islamic framework though not without Christian influences upon it, for significant minorities. But their new neighbours were different. Like the distant powers which had helped to project them into the scene, they seemed to ignore the existence of the other occupants. They bore no relation to the tiny traditional Jewish community in the area. As their numbers grew, the local people sensed the alarming shadow of coming events.

Double bind

Between the two wars and after the second, the two groups became gradually locked in a fearful dialectic. There were those among the Jews who, like Martin Buber, the philosopher, were genuine idealists and envisaged a joint Arab/Jewish state, established without conflict. There were professional people on both sides who became friends and colleagues. But the main Jewish thrust was for continually more and more settlement and acquisition of land by purchase. The British administration, mandated by the League of Nations, inherited incompatible promises made to each side and tried to introduce democratic institutions even-handedly, to totally unequal populations. Arab riots in the 1920s signalled Arab alarm.

It was the holocaust, however, which ushered in the change which was to confirm Arab fears. It changed the Jewish situation, even more the Jewish attitude, once and for all. As the Jews fled from Europe in their thousands, Canada and the United States appeared to close their doors to them. They seemed almost forced into the new 'homeland', as the one place left to them. They arrived filled with the determination that Jews would never again live entirely as guests, at the mercy of others. They would in one place be masters in their own houses.

After the Jewish population had quadrupled in four years, the Arabs saw the red light and, in 1936, they rose in revolt. They wanted to seize power before it was too late. The British response, military action followed by a commission recommending partition, was resisted by both sides. Attempts by the British to restrict the number of Jewish immigrants broke down. Meanwhile, a Jewish 'army' came to be formed and an extremist guerrilla group, the Irgun Zvai Leumi, also began to operate. Begin, later to become prime minister, began his career as an uncompromising terrorist, one of those who provided a model for the later PLO. Kenneth Cragg points the obvious parallel between him and Yassir Arafat. In 1947, the British, feeling the whole problem was getting too hot to hold, in a final evasion of responsibility handed the whole issue over to the United Nations. That body proceeded once again to recommend partition and formulate an elaborate plan.

The Palestinians were now the most bitterly aggrieved of all colonial populations, betrayed by the British, and caught up into a history stemming from events outside their world. They could not come to any kind of terms with the bitter reality of their new situation. Deprived of their expected independence, they now seemed doomed to bring a tragic fate on themselves. Their rejection of the UN partition plan, which could have given them 45% of the land, led them into desperate fighting. The Jews, militarily as in other ways better organised, were thus enabled, by the end of the war, to consolidate their holdings, taking 85% of the land instead of the 55% they had been allotted, and had originally accepted. The international community later accepted these post-1949 boundaries as those to which Israel should in theory return.

Meanwhile the massacre of the inhabitants of an Arab village, Deir Yasin, led to a panic flight of Arabs from their homes. Even the moderate Weizmann described this tragedy as 'a miraculous clearing of the land: the miraculous simplification of Israel's task', since then a sign of the prevalent Jewish attitude. Every Palestinian reaction has led to a further Palestinian setback. The total rejection of the presence of all those Jews who have come in since the 'Zionist invasion' (it is not clear which invasion is meant) has only served to intensify Jewish fear and aggression. It was Arab rhetoric and the constant violent Palestinian efforts to regain what they had lost that led to the Six-Day War. Israel, taking advantage of the international situation, finally managed to occupy the last fragment of Palestinian land. Again it was the subsequent desperate Arab recourse to Irgun Zvai Leumi methods which identified them in the minds of much of the world with 'terrorism'. It was their border raids and attacks on civilians in the 1970s which brought the Israelis into Lebanon in 1978. Finally, it was PLO military concentrations in the Lebanon which led to the Israeli invasion after a nine-month cease-fire and to what has seemed very much a kind of mass murder of Palestinians.

In defeat and exile, in the agony of homelessness, the Palestinians have indeed become what the Jews once were, a martyr people. They have been labourers in Jewish fields, vineyards, houses, but otherwise expected somehow to go elsewhere. Even Arab citizens of Israel, who have been given something of a voice and a place, seem to be there on sufferance.

The Palestinians beyond the borders have had their own sense of being a nation intensified by shared suffering. Those confined in the camps, and the more prosperous members of the wider diaspora, formed shadow institutions of the government of a future state and dwelt in imagination in a national home. Their passionate longing for their own earth, for every imagined stick and stone of it, is as vivid to them in its own way as was once for the Jews the Zionist yearning.

But what has all this done to the Jews? Outside the church of the Nativity at Bethlehem, as heavily armed soldiers tramped by with a conqueror's tread, one Jewish friend observed: 'Now, we are the Romans of the time of Jesus' birth. The Arabs are the Jews going up to the census.' The same man told me how, in the days when access to the 'wailing wall' of the Temple was restricted by the British and only two at a time might go there to pray, he felt a deep sense of the holiness of the place. Now, he said, Jewish conquest has made there a triumphant open Plaza where all may assemble for national occasions, and the 'shekinah' (the glory) has departed.

Thus intuitively he registered the feeling that Zionism has lost its soul. Of course the Jew still feels alone and misunderstood in the world. The Israelis are constrained by their perennially hostile surroundings and by a certain precarious desperation which their critics have not experienced. From the start, their attitude to their Arab neighbours, in some ways typically European in its arrogance, has been sharpened by perpetual rejection at the hands of Europe. Most of them made little attempt to relate on equal terms with the Arabs round them. Indeed, the more they themselves have broken with their former willingness to accept suffering with stoic resignation, the more they seem ready to inflict such suffering on others for the sake of their own survival.

At the heart of the life of Israel, a growing number of the more sensitive members of the community suspect that all is not well. They have been deeply concerned at the whole present policy in the occupied West Bank and Gaza. They see the increasingly ready use of gunfire, even against young children. They recognise that the same process of settlement turning into expropriation and annexation, which was used so effectively in present-day Israeli terri- tory, is now being applied increasingly on the West Bank. Finally, the invasion of Lebanon in June 1982, and the terrible slaughter of the innocents it brought in its train, aroused more minority criticism than any previous military action by Israel.

The justification for the extent of the Israeli invasion is not wholly evident. There were conflicting reports of Israeli behaviour. Whereas in some areas soldiers' lives were appar- rently jeopardised to save civilians, in others we read first- hand accounts of inexcusable brutality to civilians and prisoners, of an arrogant attitude towards the Lebanese, of people being falsely identified by hooded informers and then shot, of an Israeli soldier kicking to death a young Palestinian who asked him for water. Of course, violence once again provoked violence. The PLO have never, save in one interview given by the beleaguered Arafat, publicly acknowledged the right of Israel to exist. Palestinian guerrillas made no secret of their desire to kill as many Israelis as possible. They also tended largely, but sometimes out of necessity, to site their guns in civilian areas, even beside schools and hospitals.

Yet there was a ruthless heedlessness of the value of human life about much of Israeli tactics. In victory there was an air of brutal dominance about some of the conquerors, together with an attempt to hide from the world much of what happened, even to make it difficult to bring relief. A century after the pogroms in Russia, it all began to look more and more like a Jewish-directed pogrom. It took on something of the air of a holocaust of the Palestinians. It was an attempt, matching and in the end outweighing that of the Palestinians, to resolve by force a problem that cannot be so resolved, and to do so with the same disregard of innocent lives as all terrorists have shown. Israeli propaganda has attempted to ignore this. The official line has been to maintain complete innocence.

The fact is that Israeli and PLO supporters, in their ever-increasing hardening of attitudes towards each other, each present the other with a mirror image of utterly insensitised hatred. The 1982 invasion was the culmination of a distorting process in which many of us, especially the British, have had a hand. After the still unbelievable experience of the Jews in the concentration camps and gas chambers, it worsened. Gradually the state of Israel became the epitome of the Jewish distrust of the Gentile world. The total Jewish disregard of the Palestinian case, and reliance on the right of conquest, intensified the cause of the very insecurity which it sought to counter. The Israeli has grown into someone, as has been said, fighting the German in his dream by night as he fights in reality the Arab by day. After the terrible blow inflicted upon the Palestinians, their passionate commitment to maintain their cause and avenge the dead will not lessen. Indeed, they are likely to take refuge now in desperate hopes of achieving world attention by fresh acts of international terrorism. Their only two sources of encouragement may well be the self-defeating ineptness of the Israeli policy on the West Bank and the ever-increasing birth rate of the Arabs in both Israel itself and the occupied territories.

The Way of the Cross

For the true peace of Israel, as for the true fulfilment of the Palestinians, there is really only one way left. It is the way which first of all Westerners must be summoned to follow. The Israeli arrival in Palestine must take its place in the whole wider history of the Western encounter with the Middle East. The tragic pangs of modernisation and Western domination are among the deepest wounds of Islam. The whole present upheaval in the Middle East is part of a widespread repudiation of Western culture throughout the Third World. What is required of Westerners is a firm re-evaluation of their role in the rest of the world, of the key part they still have to play and yet of the inevitable ambivalence with which they are now bound to be regarded by others. What is required of them is not remorse or loss of nerve but a disposition very much nearer to what Christians call repentance.

Israel, itself in Arab eyes an offshoot of the West, desperately needs to discover such a disposition. Yet it has to do this without having had the benefit of the security which the rest of us have enjoyed. It may be easier for, say, the British to repent, recognising just how much responsibility they bear for the present impasse. The Israelis have suffered so much more at the hands of the very Westerners with whom they now appear to be identified. Yet a growing number of them are beginning to recognise that there must be a change of course for them also in their country. Even some of their soldiers seem to have been shaken by the terrible results of their work in the Lebanon.

Apart from the ultra-nationalists in power and their more fanatical supporters, more ordinary Israelis than ever before seem to be wearying of war. Many people in Israel itself, and in the dispersion in Europe and the United States, have been disturbed by the obvious contradictions built into the so-called 'Operation Peace in Galilee', and by having always 'to hate the Arab in the cause of peace'. Could not some way be found towards an acceptance of some real responsibility for the terrible wrongs done to Palestinian Arabs, a departure from what Kenneth Cragg calls 'the myth of innocence'? Such a change of heart would open up the possibility of relating again not only to Arabs but also to the rest of the world. The Israelis must be constrained to concede to the Palestinians the very fulfilment which they themselves have so long asked of the world, namely a 'national home'. The Palestinians must now be offered a homeland on the West Bank and the Gaza Strip. They could be now, at their moment of greatest weakness and vulnerability, open to such a gesture.

This could only happen if the Palestinians really are prepared in response to lay down their arms once and for all. It is difficult for Westerners, and especially for the British, to ask the Arabs to forgive. How, asked Winifred Coate, a CMS missionary in Jordan, can Westerners ask Palestinians to forgive 'to do something no Christian nation has ever done or been asked to do ... ?' Yet this is really the only way forward, for them as for us. The Palestinian poet, Kemal Nasir, rejected the way of Jesus.

> Apostle of forgiveness, in our tragedy,
> Neither forgiveness nor love avail ...

The whole Palestinian Arab temperament and tradition, whether Muslim or Christian, inclines Palestinians more to brood on wrongs and to dream of revenge and restitution, however impossible, rather than to come to terms with harsh reality. Could more of them come even now, as some of their compatriots inside Israel have had to do, to concede the permanent existence of the state of Israel? Could they accept a radically new accommodation?

The Christian Response

How can Christians better commend this way, and witness to its truth, than they have done so far? They have for the most part alienated the Jews by that anti-semitism which contributed over the centuries to the eventual catastrophe of the Nazi gas chambers—and they have alienated the Palestinians by their identification not only with their enemies in the Lebanon but also with the West in its whole complicity.

There has certainly been within the Western mind and imagination a great deal of ill-conceived Zionism, perhaps partly out of guilt over a co-existing anti-semitism. Could this not have been part of the mix in Balfour's consciousness that influenced his approach? Might it not now be a powerful influence in the United States? There, among the so-called 'born again', today's preoccupation with speculation on the future has spilt over into a newly-fashionable form of Christian Zionism, allegedly derived from the Bible. Stephen Travis, in his useful book *I Believe in the Second Coming of Jesus*, quotes an advertisement of the American Board of Missions to the Jews which appeared in the *New York Times*:

> If you want to know where we are in history, look at the Jewish people, they are God's timepiece and the people of prophecy ... He made a covenant with Abraham, promising a large portion of the Middle East as an inheritance for him and his descendants ... The covenant is unconditional. Just like his love ... And we, knowing who made that promise, totally support the people and land of Israel in their God-given, God-promised, God-ordained right to exist. Any person or group of nations opposed to this fight isn't just fighting Israel. But God and time itself.

The most orthodox Judaism itself, and the revived Judaism of some Hasidic sects, clearly repudiates as a blasphemy this kind of sentiment. For Jews with such a viewpoint, it is utterly wrong to identify the Israel of the

Old Testament, the covenant, with the modern, semi-secular state of Israel. Modern Israel was brought into being by all-too-human force and ingenuity. It had about it from the start more of an aura of romantic nationalism, liberalism or communism than any very definite sense of dependence on God. The land promised to Abraham, even though the promise was unconditional, can only be restored, or so the most orthodox would say, in a final, supernatural return of the Jews to their God and His Law in its fulness, when the Messiah comes. It will be the fruit of true faith and integrity.

The temptation to see in contemporary political events the fulfilment of certain Old Testament prophecies must be for Christians, as for Zionist Jews, one of the subtlest and most insidious forms of a drift into idolatry and the secularisation of the Bible. The danger of over-simple and rapid identification of biblical persons and events with what seem to be their modern counterparts is always with us. For some, the beasts and demonic forms of the Apocalypse all too easily become, say, the multinationals, and the saints are seen as liberation movements of which the Exodus becomes the archetype. For others, to the right, it seems to be flying in the face of biblical evidence not to see in the re-establishment of a nation of Israel, after two thousand years, a palpable disclosure of God's plan. The forces of light have been variously perceived as the British Empire, the United States or the revival of Israel itself. The forces of destruction translate more naturally and obviously into Russia and 'Red' China closing in with all their hosts on a restored Jerusalem.

The pop apocalyptic of Hal Lindsey, at one time a best-seller in the USA, derives its attraction partly from a contemporary longing for certainty, and an enjoyment of sensational revelations about the future. It matters little to his fans that he stands in a long line of mistaken and disappointed predictors of the End. His whole particular scheme seems to hinge at least as much on the restoration of the earthly Israel in its temporal power as on Christ himself and his coming, let alone his Church, which seems in this scheme of things to be of diminished significance.

For Christians, surely the true message of the whole Bible must be precisely the opposite. The Old Testament finds its entire fulfilment, its true exegesis, in Jesus Christ. For Christians, as for the orthodox Jews, the promises of God to Israel in the Old Testament are fulfilled when the Messiah comes. The only difference is that for the Christians the Messiah *has* come. In Jesus all the prophecies are fulfilled. His risen Body is the New Temple, his people are the New Israel. The last times have begun. Jesus saw the future opening up beyond the earthly Israel to include all those who would follow him. It was to be hoped and desired, as Paul desired, that at least a remnant of the Old Israel might turn before the fulness of the Gentiles would be gathered in. But henceforth life for Jews and Gentiles alike would move towards its end in 'the Jerusalem which is above'.

The whole New Testament demonstrates how the new covenant fulfils the old. All the prophecies once applied to the historic Israel 'after the flesh' are now to find their completion in the new universal people of God. To go back to the Old Testament prophecy and Apocalyptic, to Daniel, Zachariah or Ezekiel, and to force selected fragments from them to relate arbitrarily to current events, is to miss the whole richness of their real total significance 'in Christ'. It is the Revelation of John which has already made an inspired synthesis of all this material, drawing upon the wealth of its symbolism. The work clarifies, concentrates and focuses the variety of previous visions, with Christ and his final coming again as the central theme. Here the historic Israel no longer figures. The church is clearly the new Israel. Jesus' own foreshortened vision of a future destruction of Jerusalem (to be fulfilled in AD 70) and the End Times, in Mark 13, provides an underlying framework. It is here elaborated and reapplied. Symbolic places like 'Babylon' can mean Jerusalem, Rome and other subsequent embodiments of the world. Symbolic numbers are more signs and pointers to continual meaning than literal clues to some hidden calendar.

Be that as it may, the focal point is no longer the earthly land of Palestine. It and its sacred city, precious for its associations, have become relative. The focal point now is 'the lamb slain from the foundation of the world'. In his final coming, all the other aspects of the End referred to in the New Testament and the Old are fused into one great conflict and consummation. Meanwhile, the heart of John's message, like that of his master, is no precise prediction but the summoning of his people to follow faithfully in his way of the Cross, forsaking the ways of this world, obedient and vigilant. What is thus required of the Christians now is most certainly not to side with the earthly Israel alone, any more than with the PLO alone. What is required is that they should heed the summons of the book of Revelation and take up the cross; that they should enter into the death and resurrection love of their Lord.

Could this happen? Could there be a demonstrable revival of transcendent love in God's people in Christ in the Middle East? Christianity associated with the West appears comfortable, bourgeois and powerful, conformed to this world. Palestinian Christianity seems, understandably, desperately politicalised. The ancient churches of the Middle East are stirring but do not yet show enough real sign of being revived in love.

Here and there among all of these are those who have shown us, in the very area in which Jesus first appeared as Lord of all, the only attitude by which we can still commend his costly way—CMS missionaries like the great Winifred Coate, whose work among the refugees from Palestine in Jordan restored to them their own dignity and resources, or Stanley A. Morrison, Executive Secretary of the Near East Christian Council in 1952 who, together with Arab groups in East Jerusalem and Jewish groups in Tel Aviv, first proposed a Palestinian state on the West Bank and in Gaza. But there have been many hidden saints. The task in Beirut, wrote a Chaplain there at the height of the 1975 troubles, is 'to uphold and reverence humanity at a time when it is being desecrated on all sides . . . a humanity disfigured on the cross but also transfigured and triumphant'. That humanity broke down the barriers between Jews and Gentiles and will not tolerate sectarian selfishness wrapped in the cloak of religion. One maintains it in Beirut by 'fighting off the temptation to think of this or that people or community as a "hopeless lot"; by searching out the face of the individual among the anger of the mob ' and 'by showing the church is above all a community of hope, of spiritual regeneration and reconstruction . . . '

In the Middle East Council of Churches today you can begin to see this as they work at being a rebuilding and reconciling force. Sometimes it is those Christians least associated with resort to force or with power, people like the members of the Mennonite church from America with their 'peace testimony', who may find the readiest acceptance on both sides of the Israeli/Palestinian divide. Christian participation in reconstruction in the Lebanon, in the Palestinian search for national self-hood, and in the Israeli search for security, must spring from a recovery of the gospel of the Cross and Risen life. It must be part of a widespread renewal of humble unjudgmental faith/love in the churches, and above all in the persons, involved. If Revelation is to 'come true' and Christ's way is to become a living option in the area, it must be re-embodied in the Spirit through the life and love of ordinary Christians there until 'the Spirit and the Bride say, Come!'

Recommended Reading

Kenneth Cragg, *This Year in Jerusalem*, (Darton, Longman and Todd, 1982).

Cranford Pratt and others, *Arab-Israeli Conflict: A Christian Perspective*, (Friendship Press, New York, 1979).

Towards Understanding the Arab/Israeli Conflict, (British Council of Churches, London 1982).

Michael Christopher King, *The Palestinians and the Church*, (Commission on Inter-Church Aid, Refugee and World Service WCC, Geneva, 1948–1956).

Stephen H. Travis, *I Believe in the Second Coming of Jesus*, (Hodder and Stoughton, 1982).
Jean Landouses, *Le Don de la Terre de Palestine*, (Publications CEMO, Beirut, Lebanon, 1978).
T. Boersma, *Is the Bible a Jigsaw Puzzle ... An Evaluation of Hal Lindsey's Writings*, (Christian World Publication, 12 Forrest Road, Edinburgh, EH1 2QN).
John Sweet, *Revelation*, (SCM Pelican Commentaries, SCM Press, 1979).

PART II

Entering Another's World

Word Out of Silence

One person who often comes to my mind when I think about our common task is a remarkable man whom I sometimes used to sit next to in the college where I once worked. He was a well-known biochemist: an elderly man, small, white-haired, with a certain gentle gravity about him, and a detachment from his surroundings which were impressive. He would sit amid the buzz of conversation at the high table, calmly considering some thought of his own. But, most courteously, if he noticed you were not already involved, he would turn his whole head and shoulders towards you with a gentle enquiring gaze. In fact he may have been very slightly hard of hearing and so forced to attend a little more carefully than most. But I don't think it was just that. There was in his intent expression just that hint of humorous sympathy which served to put you entirely at your ease. And yet it was a searching, penetrating look. It gave you a little of the feeling of being under some kind of therapeutic ray!

He would ask a few small seemingly simple, questions as to what you had been doing or thinking about, questions which brought out of you answers you would never really have thought of giving. It was the kind of conversation which reveals you to yourself. They remained with you, those questions, and went on sparking off surprising little flashes. He seemed to communicate his own freedom, his own relaxed alertness.

Once he remarked to me that all scientists were now touching on the edge of a mystery. And I remember thinking, yes, that is just the awareness you have always conveyed. You have spoken so relatively little. And yet you have said so much. Your words and your silences arose out of some kind of fulness. When we left you we always felt the better for your company.

Quality of being

The memory brings to mind a whole widespread movement of the Spirit flowing gradually through and beyond the Church of our time in so many areas of the world. It is a gently pervasive patterning of light and shadow, of sound and quiet, throwing out its reflection on its surroundings. Suddenly you realise that it is there, changing the whole character of the scene like the swelling of floodwaters that make their appearance unobtrusively in the night and come with the morning.

There is a new mode of mission very much nearer in its outworking to the steady spread of Christian life and community in Roman times. It is a mode more appropriate to this period than some of the ways of western Christendom in recent centuries. Once more when we hear the familiar words of the great commission of Jesus 'Go, make disciples of all nations … ' we are led to lay the stress not so much on the going but on the original heart of the sentence 'make disciples'. And where in St John's Gospel the other version of that commission occurs, 'As the Father has sent me, even so I send you …', the stress falls less on outward activity and more on an inward quality, a sensitive responsiveness to the Sender, a readiness to move or to wait, to speak or to be still. The call to mission becomes even less of a warrant for aggressive activity, let alone for a pentagon-like strategy of world dominion. Rather it is the theme of little, ever more widely scattered cells and groups, outwardly powerless, inwardly growing and through that growth attracting others. Gently, unexpectedly, they are disclosed to those to whom it is given to perceive them rightly, as at least clues to the true centre, touches of new creation, offering occasional glimpses of the possibility of a new mankind.

Out in the desert near Cairo at Wadi Latrun, I saw

something of a paradox. The Church comes nearest to meeting the essential needs of a ramshackle, rapidly expanding city beset by all the familiar problems of a third-world economy, when it appears as a transcendent mystery, demonstrating a new way of being. It offers not only a purpose for struggling individuals, young men grappling with a welter of new experience and aspiration; not only an ethic for a disrupted society in the throes of transition. It offers in the good news about Jesus and his Cross and Resurrection a resolution to the fundamental problems of personal existence; change in the very nature of man's individual and social nature; a new relationship to himself, to others, to the whole of life.

We bumped over the desert track from the main road towards the plain barrack-like outer wall, from which only tiny slits of what could be windows looked out across the endless sand dunes. I had no idea what we should find. Once parked beside the coaches, which had come out from the city packed with pilgrims, we entered a low doorway and before us was a wide court, an ordered garden with monuments to the work of former Coptic inhabitants within it. There was the original little desert stronghold of beleaguered monks, like a keep with a bridge that could be drawn up to save them from marauders and oppressors, with churches that went down in layers to pre-Islamic times. All around were newly built balconies and the windows of a new population of residents and visitors looking down. Here and there groups from the coaches stood round one or two of the young monks murmuring. The only thing the enclosure had in common with the surrounding desert was the stillness and space from which it had all sprung, to which it had all given new content.

Upstairs a young architect, one of the fifty or so graduates who had been drawn to this place to join Matthew the Poor, the refounder, spoke to us. 'We are living a miracle here,' he said. How else should Christians live? he seemed to be implying. He poured out the story of the development and then of the spread back into Cairo of the steady flame of its life through personalities and congregations. It was clearer and clearer that the magnetic attraction of the message of men like the Patriarch of the Coptic Church addressing thousands of young people weekly in his cathedral, or Fr Zechariah in Heliopolis drawing hundreds of young Christians, Muslims and agnostics to his Bible school, was at heart a quality of life in God. The message had its source and spring in this silence. What we encountered within and behind the words was a wordless way of being and of quiet practical action, as they planted and built in the burning sun and sand. The Copts had clung to their own hidden life for so long that now it had to be rediscovered among the half-ruins. It was as though some ancient seeds had been replanted and freshly watered to flower with a strange strength. What would we learn if this could happen among all the Arab Christians in the Middle East and among the other ancient oriental Churches everywhere?

In the streets of the expanding cities of the world, a flotsam and jetsam of young people swept along in a flux of new ambitions and aspirations are searching, for jobs, for recognition, for meaning. If only they could find something, someone, as powerful as this which attracted and held these young men here. All they need to be able to stumble upon is the same root that flowers here, the sign, the clue, the blossom in the wilderness that speaks of new creation as much by the depths of its quiet as by anything said.

In the presence of such a quietness every detail stands out as clearly as here in the desert light. At such a point of concentration of peace, familiar things recover that essential strangeness which analysis can never exhaust. Every particle of life is restored to something of its true relation to every other. Something of the inward 'deep-down things' is brought into awareness.

To go back from here into the endearing chaos of life in Cairo is to carry this reorientation with you. People who have learnt to live in the rhythms of this grace can be endued with such a fresh closeness to others and a fresh difference from others that those around them can be both drawn and stirred. They may sense a quality of sympathy, an atmosphere of reassurance, gentle, quite unfanatical, entirely natural. And yet there is a distance, a detachment which is so free from the normal habitual distortions of our self-seeking, that it seems the very secret of humanity and humaneness itself. It is what man was made for, and that is the very reason why it draws others so magnetically to its source.

Mode of mission
This is an intrinsic attribute of real faith in Christ wherever it is found. And it is frequently expressed in an alternation of true word and silence. The early African Christian leaders of the last 200 years were men and women of little formal education often but of great wisdom. One of the marks of those pioneers and founders of great movements and Churches all over Africa was that again and again they were described as people of few but effective words. There was an authority about them and a dignity as well as a gentleness. The early founders in the Western Delta of Nigeria were depicted to me by those who recalled them as people with a great peace and quietness. The secret of their indefatigable energy was their ability to hold that peace, as they moved long distances through the bush, entering a new village, trekking on from one perilous situation to another in the confidence of the message they had to bring.

   And so, too, in time of persecution, that peace still prevailed. The Kikuyu martyrs in Kenya, those lorry-loads of men and women who with such serenity and radiance went to their deaths in Rwanda; Simon Kimbangu, leader of a great independent Church, dying in jail in the Congo; the numberless martyrs of Uganda—all these lived out the passion in which they were given to share with their Master the same patience and quiet forgivingness in the face of false accusers. They were faithful to the pattern at the heart of the tradition according to which 'He was oppressed and afflicted yet he opened not his mouth . . . and as sheep before her shearers is dumb so he opens not his mouth'; '. . . who when he was reviled, reviled not again, when he suffered, threatened not, but committed himself to him that judges righteously . . . '

Perhaps we all need opposition and harassment to humble us and quiet us, and to teach us to put more weight of experience behind our words. After centuries of easy talking from a position of assured strength, our first line of defence in the face of criticism has sometimes tended to give some substance to E.M. Forster's jibe about 'poor, talkative little Christianity'. In countries where it is still a punishable crime to become a Christian, little, unsuppressible groups are multiplying with little help or support from any earthly power.

In the face of harsh family or social opposition and ostracism, Christians in a world in which they have less and less external protection are learning, as they had to learn before the days of western dominance, the true cost of faithful believing and witnessing. Behind the Iron Curtain, even in Russia itself, nothing less than a quiet, unostentatious spiritual renewal is growing. In China too the same unobtrusive but deep-rooting joyful faith is being secretly passed from heart to heart and tiny house-group to tiny group. The way such a faith is encountered and caught in such a setting is necessarily as much a matter of living and of deep encounter as of speaking. There will indeed be long and profound talk and marvellous writings. But these will well up out of a heart and mind which have to be full to overflowing until the right point comes at which that fulness can be embodied in word and act.

In an increasingly secular and pluralist world, faiths and ideologies of all kinds jostle together, and the war of words intensifies. We have so much to receive from those who learn to take their place alongside others, to sympathise with them, to confirm them in all that is good. In so doing such people are often given an opportunity to point beyond themselves to the One from whom they draw their own strength.

Travelling groups of young people from Taizé have been living out the theme of their Council of Youth in just this spirit. In Bangladesh, in the Philippines and in Indonesia the *Letter from Taizé* (July–August 1977) describes them sharing and praying with fellow Christians but also drawing alongside all people of all faiths and kinds.

> Under a road bridge, a group of people—sisters, a brother from Taizé, students, young workers—sit and share a meal with families who have here their only home. The bridge is their roof, and their floor a few planks placed in the water . . .

There are long times of listening

> . . . sharing each other's experience of struggle and suffering and each other's visions of hope. Listening to words spoken by workers at grips with situations of injustice, where those who speak out lose their job; by people working for the release of political prisoners . . .

In Java they celebrated Easter by visiting the sick, eating shared gifts of food, talking and praying with village families.

These youngsters, with their free spirituality of listening, sharing and rejoicing with others, are evidence of a new stirring of the Spirit. After the first shock of industrialisation and city life, and of the melting down of all the old cultural forms into one pot, we can begin to sense preparations for a recasting, the emergence of a new stage. In many parts of the world in the last hundred years the Church came to be part of a highly articulate, imposed and alien framework, often in a middle-class setting, often with an air of unconscious superiority about it. As we renounce false self-assertion, the lesson of the Cross will be learnt again and the sovereignty of God in Christ will shine forth again, without depending on our over-garrulous defence.

It is like the message that came to the poet R.S. Thomas, alone in a solitary moonlit church.

In cities that
have outgrown their promise people
are becoming pilgrims
again; if not to this place,
then to the recreation of it
in their own spirits. You must remain
kneeling. Even as this moon
making its way through the earth's
cumbersome shadow, prayer, too,
has its phases . . .

'Be still and know . . . stand still, and see the salvation of
the Lord . . . ' The new phase is being born out of a
willingness to be humbled, to trust and to wait, a willingness to listen and patiently abide, to serve, to share and
above all to love with a supernatural love.

Gift of the Spirit
The most telling description I know of this quality of spirit
is Ivan Illich's marvellous essay on 'The Eloquence of
Silence' in his *Celebration of Awareness*, surely one of the
best things he has ever written. Interestingly enough it
arose out of an attempt to prepare people who were going
to work as 'missionaries' among Puerto Ricans in Spanish
ghettos in New York. At the outset Illich comments on the
spiritual discipline of truly learning a foreign language.

Properly conducted language learning is one of the few
occasions in which an adult can go through a deep
experience of poverty, of weakness and of dependence on
the goodwill of another.

As if in recognition of the significance of what they were
doing, students gathered every evening for an hour of
silent prayer, and this essay was a meditation offered at
the beginning of one such hour.

The speaker saw language itself as 'a pattern of noises
and pauses, like electrons in the atom, planets, luminous
points in space', a cord of silence with sounds as the knots.

This is the point. The learning of a language thus becomes 'even more the learning of its silences than its sounds'. And 'it takes more effort and delicacy to learn the silence of a people than its sounds'. And missionaries so often 'never come to speak properly' to receive the intimate gift the people have to give them, to communicate sensitively through silences. They never master the 'yang/yin', the complementary rhythms of utterance and pause. Thus 'they remain forever thousands of miles away'. 'Silences can only be acquired through a delicate openness to them.'

The meditation goes on to look at the varieties of 'class' in the grammar of silence, different kinds of silence. There is the silence before words, the silence which prepares for them and 'within which words live or die'. There is the silence beyond words which comes when there is no more that can be said and which can be either of heaven or of hell, where it becomes the stony silence of isolation, always a threat to missionary existence.

> In fact, with the unusual possibilities of witnessing through silence, unusual ability to destroy through it is open to the man charged with the word in a world not his own.

There is a danger of sullenness, or of numb, mute despair. But at the opposite pole lies 'the silence of love, the holding of the hands of the lovers ... the form of communication which opens the simple depth of the soul'. It comes in flashes and can become a lifetime—in prayer just as much as with people. Perhaps it is the only truly universal aspect of language, the only means of communication which was not touched by the curse of Babel. Perhaps it is the one way of being together with others and with the Word in which we have no more 'foreign accent'.

Finally there is the silence of a kind of dying to self, a kind of handing over of oneself, which the author calls 'the silence of the *pieta*', because it is a silence 'beyond bewilderment and questions ... beyond the possibility of an answer or even reference to a word which preceded'. It is the silence of utter self-giving. The 'mysterious silence through which the Lord could descend into the silence of hell, the acceptance without frustration of a life, useless and wasted on Judas, a silence of freely willed powerlessness through which the world was saved'.

Right the way through, the essay draws its analogies between our silence with men and with God. It sees this as the secret of all that I have been talking about. 'To learn the full meaning of the one we must practise and deepen the other'. The Christian believes in the Word as co-eternal with silence. And it is in the prayer of silent listening that we acquire the habit of that pure attention through which the message of the other becomes 'he in us'. By means of such silence the Virgin was enabled to become 'the eternal model of openness to the Word', through which we could take flesh. 'The silence of the city priest on the bus listening to the report of the sickness of a goat is a gift, truly the fruit of a missionary form of long training in patience'. Indeed all the good silences are seen as a form of prayer, 'the slow prayer of hesitation' or the still prayer of the practice of the presence.

To be able to be silent in this way is a gift of the Spirit. I could not be writing of it if I did not believe this, at least only with the same self-contradiction with which it is said that Carlyle 'wrote forty volumes in praise of silence'! The Lord of all language gives speech in tongues, I know, but, equally for the humanly taciturn and the verbose alike, 'the silent and the garrulous liars', his quietness of heart and mind must come as a gift of love. It must be of that same kind of expectancy and awe which prevailed when 'there was silence in heaven for the space of about half an hour'. (That half an hour signifies one of those recurring breaks by which the apocalypse continually rises to its great symphonic climax.) It partakes of that silence which all the earth keeps before the presence of the Lord in the Old Testament (Habbakuk 2.20) and the thick darkness which went before him and which he makes his secret place.

In Eastern Christian tradition, the man who prays in the Spirit, his mind in his heart, and in whom the rhythm of the Jesus prayer has established itself, is drawn like Moses on Mount Sinai, into this silence not of word but of thought. People often write and speak of 'mystical experience' as if in all 'faiths' it were essentially the same thing, a curiously Hindu way of thinking. But just at the point in Christian faith where you might expect all religions to converge, in a silence beyond word and thought, you find in fact that nothing is further from the truth. There are after all, as the Illich essay makes clear, many varieties of silence.

The silence of Christian prayer at this, its centre, has little in common with the silence of that entry into the abyss of the one which is nothing and everything, the monad of which Hinduism and even Sufism speak, the self-loss of Buddhist nirvana. No. This is much more akin to Illich's 'silence of lovers'. It is a wordless *communion* (as against union) in which man does not cease to be creature nor forgiven sinner even when he participates in the divine life. The One who receives him does so with the wounded hands of Creator and Redeemer. No wonder that, over against the Platonists, the Eastern fathers jealously guarded the concreteness of the Personal Being of God. Only through the Cross could man be brought into this relationship with him.

A man can be drawn into God's presence and love and held there, the heart silent and open, in tears and in a prayer which even while it speaks the name of Jesus turns away from every external thought or image. Every presence of man before the face of God is a prayer. Thought and emotion fail and fall short, language and concept are broken in the encounter with the living God 'through Jesus Christ' in the Spirit. He transcends all unity or variety of being in which he allows men to share with him.

Silence becomes penitence and humbling death and resurrection. 'It is a great thing to speak of God but still better to purify oneself before God.' The Jesus prayer keeps central that concrete personal forgiveness and compassion by which God enters into our life as we enter into his. It drives us back into the need and suffering of his world and into our whole involvement with every one of our fellow beings. The closer we come to the cleansing liberation and affirmation of God's presence with us, the closer we are drawn to all other men and beasts and created things. We begin to become part of the New Man, the new world in Christ which, since it is of the future, transcends all expression to God and to all things of which in this life only tongues or silence can speak.

Heart to heart

For while all things were in quiet silence and night was in the midst of her swift course, Thine Almighty word leapt down from Heaven . . .

The ministry of both speech and silence, of God's word out of silence, becomes the perfect medium through which the Spirit can enable us to convey the cleansing, the healing and the re-affirming which we have ourselves received. The more freely we go on receiving, the more freely we will be enabled to give. And we shall find ourselves sometimes at least able to communicate more when we refrain from speaking and wait for others to discover and articulate the secret for themselves. Essentially this is a disposition which refuses to dominate or manipulate others but is content to offer them the resources for their own growth. It is both humility and tender appreciation of the potential of other people, without which all community work is in vain. Illich was giving us the spirituality which alone would make his own approach to education and healing possible. It is the spirituality for a Church once again breaking beyond the confines of the institutions and social groupings in which it was tended to become imprisoned. It is the spirituality for a Church which is once again growing into a pervasive movement, a humane conspiracy, standing always and everywhere at the side of the deprived, the exploited and the excluded.

So that what I have been describing is not just some kind of rarefied hobby for the mystically minded. It is eminently practical. It is the supreme means through which we can be given grace to work with people. This quality of listening is essential to our total ministry and not least to the whole attempt to enable every group of people, especially the seemingly disadvantaged, to find their own resources for healing, teaching and ministering to each other. They need not then depend so much upon others but discover their interdependence. It is the secret of the principle of 'self-reliance', perhaps better termed 'mutual reliance'.

People in community development of one kind or another so often have all the right theory. In one project the director lectured one all the way to the village on the principle of encouraging people to discover and voice their own needs, letting them make their own plans and learn confidence in their own capacity. But once arrived at the site it was clear that he was still really giving all the orders and ultimately making all the choices and decisions. He didn't really seem able to listen for what was unsaid. The truth is this style of work demands much more than good theory. It requires costly practice, a sympathy, a patience, a humility—even, ideally, a deep capacity for self-effacement and the encouragement of others

and of the best leaders
when the work is complete
the people will say
we did it ourselves ...

to quote Mao Tse-tung. So often non-directiveness is but old directiveness writ large. The 'enabler' is such a strong personality that everyone in fact looks to him.

Consider what was required for effectiveness in the marvellous experiments described by Roy Billington in *Health, a Surprising Joy*, so full of good stories, in the chapter entitled 'Unsuspected human riches'.

As people are treated 'like human beings', that is, with respect and with appreciation for what they have to give, even in a prison wing for life-sentence men, in an old people's home, in communities for the subnormal or mentally handicapped, they come to life. In the old people's home, for instance, a teacher came in to work with six bedridden women patients, suffering from confusion, loss of memory and incontinence and statistically likely to die soon. His aim was to make their lives richer and happier by re-creating personal identity, redeveloping personal responsibility and encouraging them to remember past events. The nurses were encouraged to talk to and listen to the patients all the time. They had papers and magazines read to them, recalled similar happenings in their own experience. They cooked, laid tables, wrote letters, played games and were all the time attended to. Every little task was a chance for discussion, and encouragement of initiative. The room was brightened. Patients chose clothes, the menu, the pictures. Within eight weeks they were moving about the ward. Incontinence stopped. After six months no one had died and standards of dressing, food preparation, conversation and independence were very satisfactory. 'Now I look with seeing eyes on old age,' said the teacher, Frank Parker, headmaster of Craven Lodge School, Melton Mowbray.

The same approach is widely and desperately required to meet the problems and needs of so many of us the world over. Rural development, says Peter Batchelor, founder of Faith and Farm in West Africa, means living among people, sitting down humbly and listening to them, until with the passing of time conversation becomes less reserved and trust comes. It means forbearance of a kind which is prized and recognized in cultures 'where impatience is much more of a sin than it is in the western world'.

One suspects the same spiritual calibre is being required in many such situations, a quality of long-suffering, of gentleness, of goodness, which cannot be rapidly manufactured and through which the words a man speaks will be heard, the things he cares about can be shared.

'Do you mind if they try to evangelise?' I asked the director of a community association in the inner city when some of those preparing for mission were going to work

with him. 'Not if they earn the right to do so,' he replied.
Later he explained to them what he meant. In all social
work we have to draw alongside others at a level at which
we ourselves are ready to learn and expose ourselves
enough to be able to be wounded. Heart speaks to
heart—*cor ad cor loquitur*. And sooner or later whatever
you have in you comes through.

The silence of love again. 'It comes in flashes and can
become a lifetime—in prayer just as much as with people
... ' Perhaps that was all that was needed to be said!

Recommended Reading

R.S. Thomas, *Laboratories of the Spirit*, (Macmillan, 1975).
Peter G. Batchelor, *Christians and Rural Development*, (Tear
Fund, Teddington, 2nd ed., 1976).
Roy Billington, *Health, a Surprising Joy*, (CMS, 1976).
V. Lossky, *The Mystical Theology of the Eastern Church*, (James
Clarke, Cambridge, 1957).
Kallistos Ware, 'Silence in Prayer' in *Theology and Prayer*, A. M.
Allchin (ed.) (Fellowship of St Alban and St Sergius, 1975).
Letter from Taizé, published monthly. English edition c/o 23
Christie Street, Dunfermline, Fife, Scotland, or 2150 Almaden
Road 114, San Jose, Ca. 95125, USA.

Point of Balance

The right human face
When I meet a friend whom I haven't seen for some time and he asks me what I am doing now, my answer often leads on into other questions: What do you Christians think you have to bring to the human situation today? What in fact do you think you have to give? And I find that, as I grope for an answer, the picture of a face forms in my mind. And yet it isn't exactly one face. Rather, it's a similar expression that I have glimpsed in many faces; faces scattered across the world, faces different in physiological make-up and different in colour, faces from a whole variety of climates and cultures. These faces have differing facial languages, so to speak, and yet all of them have conveyed unmistakably the same message. Within each human encounter has been transmitted an essentially identical central reassurance. *The right human face*, Edwin Muir described it precisely in writing of the face of his beloved:

> Yes, yours, my love, is the right human face
> I in my mind had waited for this long,
> Seeing the false and searching for the true,
> Of welcome suddenly amid the wrong
> Valleys and rocks and twisting roads . . .

It is a kind of welcome home, a sense of rightness, humane and humorous, wise with its own knowledge, its own implicit proportion, its own essential moderation.

Moderation is much talked about in our particular

society in a way that suggests a rather amiable, muddled pragmatism which, it is hoped by those who invoke it, is still somehow characteristically British. But it can be something much more than an agreeable compromise which those of no very clear conviction seem pleasantly able to arrive at together. It can be that strangely rare and iron-hard quality, a real reconciliation of opposites. It can be that energy of the Spirit, which, as Bishop Dehqani put it, 'flows from the combination of negative and positive'. It can consist of differences that are genuinely held together in a costly integrity. A childhood friend had a maxim, 'Pursue the moderate course violently': That is a hard pursuit, until you find a moderation that pursues you, that will grasp you, if you can let it, in that lovely balance, the equipoise of grace.

One face that impressed me with its juxtaposition of opposed qualities miraculously fused was that of Mother Teresa in Calcutta. Characteristically, it seemed to reflect 'as in a glass' the mystery it so often contemplates, 'Only draw your love,' she said, 'from a deep enough source and sooner or later those whom you love will recognise where it comes from.'

I think that this quality of moderation and the meeting of contrasting attributes is the essential quality of personal love, a deeply healing virtue, a salve for body and spirit and, for that matter, for society. I believe you can arrive at a clearer description of it through looking at some of these contrasts.

Meeting point of universal and particular
Take, for instance, one such combination that always characterises the personal love of which Mother Teresa spoke—that of the particular and the universal. The face of love is always marked by both. It is sculpted out of particular material by particular circumstances and yet it speaks a transcultural language. It belongs to a specific time and place and setting and yet it appears always and everywhere significant, offering a homecoming to men of all faiths or of none. An old Hindu man in the little lobby

where we awaited Mother Teresa prostrated himself with the respect he felt due to all forms of holiness. Here was a reality that included and met all men whatever their religion or race. And yet that very reality owes its particular and distinctive quality to the fact that Mother Teresa has sensed herself possessed by a strongly personal love, rooted in a particular concrete personal history, bearing the marks of a particular death and a particular life and of the personal Spirit that sprang out of the heart of that life in death. It is this personal love which gives force and meaning to her whole life so that as she would put it, she and her sisters live 'in him' and 'he in them'.

Stanley Jones wrote to Gandhi: 'I think you have grasped the principles of the Christian faith but you have missed the Person. May I suggest you penetrate the principles to the Person . . . ?'

Geoffrey Paul in a sermon to CMS expressed it in a similar way:

We have to say that the gospel is not essentially about attitudes or actions arising from following Jesus Christ— about love, respect or justice. It is about Jesus himself for his own priceless worth. We preach the gospel when we introduce men to the source from which Love and Justice spring, when we tell them of One who is able to set them free from within.

And it is precisely those who sense themselves grasped by such a particular freedom who seem enabled to gain such a universal response.

I was amazed to find in Peshawar, for instance, on the North West Frontier of Pakistan, that a Christian psychiatrist and medical social workers coming from Britain were getting through to Pathan tribesmen. They would bring some struggling mentally deranged relative into the hospital. In the welcoming atmosphere of a ward run partly by one of the man's own countrymen, and with the sympathetic attention of one of the team, the violence was removed. It might be seen by the relatives as a miracle.

But what was ministered was real love, a distinterested concern for his need which the patient perceived. And the message as to the source of such a love comes through, as the doctor has put it, 'at an unconscious level where it arouses no defensive reaction, but, bypassing cultural difference, transcending language or concept, does its quiet work at the level of the heart'.

Distance and nearness
Take another contrast in the face of love, the feeling of what I will call distance and nearness. The closer it is to us, the further away it still seems to be.

> . . . the sweet presence of a good diffused
> And in diffusion ever more intense . . .

That very paradox was perfectly expressed to me by an Indian friend as we came out from seeing Mother Teresa. 'Isn't she marvellous? She makes you feel bigger *and* smaller at the same time'. Such a presence always gives you a sense that you are of value. You have access to the other person, with whom you can relax and respond fully. But at the same time, there is a difference about that other person which confronts you, fights with you against the betrayer within you ('Get thee behind me Satan'!) and so, by its very opposition, 'confirms' you, as Buber puts it, in being more truly yourself. In Jesus there is this accessibility and yet a strange remoteness. The disciples are at home and yet in awe. But this very juxtaposition is characteristic of all personal being and of all real love. I believe we encounter it at its fullest in the faces of those who reflect Jesus.

Strength and vulnerability
In another way you can see this quality as a fusion of power and of gentleness—so often found in the faces of men and women deeply imprinted with Christ's love. Sundhar Singh, for instance, or the Ugandan Apolo Kivebulaya, or the extraordinary blend of independence of

mind and humility in the face of Teilhard de Chardin, or the hauntingly diffident firmness of Samuel Crowther whose face gazes across the hall in our College at Selly Oak named after him. It is there in the larger-than-life statue of Edward King who bends down towards you in the transept of Lincoln Cathedral, surprising you as you look up with a gleam of what almost seems to be mutual recognition, as he peers humorously into you, and you remember the text he loved: 'Thy gentleness hath made me great.' As Owen Chadwick said of that face, 'no one could think that it reflected the gentleness of weakness or insignificance; it was the gentleness of a controlled strength.'

Here is the insight that, through the 'self-emptying' of Jesus sees the ultimate sovereignty of the Divine residing in a willingness to be made vulnerable. How striking that both Kemal Hussein of Cairo and more recently Dr Hassan Askari, representatives of a faith that most emphasises God's transcendent power, discover in the Cross a potential theology of weakness. It is one of the main themes of Kenneth Cragg's whole endeavour to explore the contrast between the triumphant pilgrimage of the Prophet to Mecca and the journey of Jesus up to Jerusalem to face death.

Justice and compassion

But this again shades into a greater combination still, that of justice and compassion. It is another characteristic of the kind of faces I have mentioned. Here is the shrewd homeliness, the searching appreciativeness of a gaze which has no reservations but also no illusions. It cherishes you too much to be deflected. It is both astute and fundamentally innocent, serpent and dove. It is what Gustav Aulen called 'love with its eyes open'.

Iris Murdoch wrote of art: 'The realism of the great artist is not a photographic realism, it is essentially pity and justice.' The terrible clarity and tenderness with which Solzhenitsyn explores the predicament of all his characters, even Stalin himself, is a case in point. His vision recognises evil for what it is, refuses sentimentality, endures a tragic

view of life with irony as well as a deeply-torn tenderness
and thus ultimately discloses the possibility of some kind
of wholeness. But I do not believe that such a wholeness
can ever in the end be attained without our coming at last
to the one all-inclusive tragedy—and comedy—the Divine
Comedy, the central point at which life is given final form
and meaning: Jesus himself. 'Righteousness and peace and
mercy and truth have kissed each other' and been made
commensurate at the last. We cannot *dare*, I believe, to
draw upon any hallower source than this if we are
struggling to seek to meet the world's infinite need at
whatever level—social, political, individual and always
ultimately personal. The source must be the Cross.

Realism and idealism
We begin to find other reconciliations reflected in the face
of those who live out of that Cross. It opens up the
foundation for a marriage of ideals and scepticism, of
realism and hope. Our world increasingly alternates
between waves of exhilarated but unreal expectation of
change (even in the Church people find it possible to live on
excitement) and then troughs of depression and disillusionment. In societies all over the world young people are
grasping for change, with little to lose and much to long
for, and there can be intense utopian fervour alongside a
sardonic cynicism and a fear of being hurt. Those who work
among the poor in our own inner cities and all over the
Third World experience daily the crushing weight of weary
bewilderment and disappointment.

The poor, of course, have so much to teach us about this
balance of grace, if we are willing to learn from them. A
friend who lives in Asia described how, after a landslip had
robbed a man of his parents, his wife and children, he wept
and cried out: 'Why? Why should this happen to us on
whom everything falls?'

But later, after the day's pain, some of the people were
celebrating a festival and my friend went out with them to
'dance in the sea' as they call it, the night calm, the moon
out, the water full of chattering children. The marvellous

resilience of the poor. It brought back a surer hold on resurrection.

On the other hand, in the most perfectly ordered societies, there must be room for weakness, a relaxed sense of the vast gap between ideal and reality. As D. H. Lawrence said of the novel 'there is always a banana skin somewhere on the premises'. There is a scope for irony and a proper recognition of our continuing incongruity. There is a call for those who can rejoice with those that rejoice and weep with those that weep, or who, with Mozart, in Barth's picture of him 'hear the sad music of humanity *within* the joyful music of the great unguessed-at finale'. How many a face, full of faith and fire, set towards the adventure of mission and service, has been etched over the years with the inner knowledge which love must bear, not only of the power of resurrection, but also of the fellowship of suffering?

Material and spiritual
And such a face can be neither wholly the face of the mystic, the spiritual man so-called, nor wholly that of the materialist. So much of our culture, and indeed of the world's flux of cultures, tends to shatter into one of these two alternatives, romantic or rationalist, dreamer, aesthetic, unpractical rebel or technician.

To reject the form, hierarchy and continuity of history for the immediate, the communal and the spontaneous may be self-defeating. The cult of the intuitive, the imaginative, the emotional, the Earth Mother, is falsely set against the male, the intellectual, the calculative, for each in truth needs the other. People begin to move from one a little nearer to the other as they begin to come to grips with the *whole* of reality. They are groping then towards the fully personal, the poise which ultimately only grace can give. This will hold them from giving way to great disillusionment as confidence in the transformation of life breaks up under the weight of disappointment.

The 'Dilaram' communities of Kabul and Delhi have been offering such a recovery of genuinely personal, incarnate life to the hippies who have wandered in there off the trails of India or Nepal. I visited one of these houses. Of the spirituality there's no doubt. There's an aerial feeling of colour and light and freedom which fits the pilgrim's quest. It is all tenderness and sensitive caring, gentle and open. But running through it all there is also a sharpness and clarity, a firmness. The washing up is to be done and 'he that will not work cannot eat'. There are others and oneself to come to terms with. This is not the spirituality of the escape from the material.

It is that very interrelation which Nayantara Sahgal explores so perceptively in *The Day in Shadow* where the heroine, Simri, feeling back to her Hindu past, passive and dazed by her painful divorce from her materialist, go-getter husband, feels that all that is left to her of her own spiritual tradition is formless and amorphous, lacking direction. Can Raj, the son of an over-westernised Christian, with an inherited singlemindedness, a purposeful zest and drive, offer her a way forward? Their interplay epitomises the struggle of so many people—in their half-worlds, their broken cultures—to find integration and healing, a practical revival, a spirit-born impulse that moves through the political and the social and offers another possibility for man.

Becoming the Son of Man

Every Advent and every Christmas draw us onward through the shortened days and the closing in of the dark, towards a border country, a country where opposites may mingle, a no-man's land that belongs to every man. In our search for a fundamental purpose and meaning in the world, a true shape to society, and adequate forms of thought and feeling and personal life, we can I believe be grasped and led, if we would go willingly to the place where creatures are humbled to receive a power which meets their need. This power meets the needs of disintegrated societies, changing religions, fragmentary and seemingly inconsequential lives, because they are essentially the needs of persons. And it is a personal love which can heal and recreate, and carry us through and beyond the contradictions of finitude and death into a boundless future, as together in the mysterious phrase of the Gospel we 'become the Son of Man'.

The possibility is opened up that men may have bestowed upon them the mastery and freedom of grace. It lightens the faces of those who discover its mysterious balance until they themselves begin to reflect the ultimate reintegration of 'the Glory of God in the face of Jesus Christ'.

Recommended books

Nayantara Sahgal, *The Day in Shadow* (Vikas Publications, 64 Ladbroke Grove, London, W11, 1971).

Response to Islam
I: Points of Entry

In these next two chapters we will consider carefully the quality of our response to the world of Islam. In the end, our ways into each other's worlds lie essentially through personal encounters and hard-won friendships, through costly feeling and perceiving. The thought brings to my mind a few of the rich variety of encounters you can have once you begin to explore. In this chapter I propose to sketch one or two of them, and in the next chapter to think more about their implications.

A high tower
A dark staircase comes first to mind—a staircase by which you stumble your way up to a deep-set, shuttered room. Through the chinks you can just tell that you are perched above a Middle Eastern city. A famous Muslim scholar sits gently in his office. He has the kind of authority and freedom tempered by humble courtesy of men who know what to do with their solitude. At first you feel ashamed of the hurried superficiality of your life. But he soon disarms you, handing you a cup with the kind of unguarded smile he might have reserved for an old friend.

In so many ways his outlook—honest, balanced, humane —is just what you would covet for yourself. It is this that gives even more force to his words, impressing them deeply upon you. 'By and large, you Christians have not *loved* us. You have come claiming to love us, but quite outside our culture and apart from the things which make us what we are. You claim to respect us and care for us as people, yet you in fact ignore or despise the themes and forms that shape us. How can this be? What kind of love is this?'

It is the echo of an old cry which has rung out down the thirteen or fourteen centuries of distortion in our relations with Islam. Even at the time of Muhammad's first vision in a cave near Mecca, in which the angel Gabriel revealed himself first as a voice, then as a fiery figure astride the horizon, the potential range of the Prophet's vision had already been violently restricted. He had been searching far-sightedly beyond the failing tribal divinities of a crumbling nomadic society—searching for a moral order, a faith that would match the needs also of merchants in new urban centres, feeling for a wider world—searching ultimately for a personal God and a new universal community. But the cruelty and treachery of Byzantium, the Hellenes' ill-treatment of Arab Christians, had so identified Christianity with perfidy and injustice that the Christian empire itself virtually blotted out the faintest hope of Muhammad's discerning at the heart of the radiance of his vision the form of 'one like to the Son of Man'. From that day to this the behaviour of the majority of Christians has put up the same barriers of arrogance and pride.

But from the beginning there have always been those on both sides who have broken through to each other, and our scholar friend was one of these, summoning us to join himwith a profoundly humane reasonableness. He was speaking as a kind of Erasmus among Muslims, breathing, with all his learning, all his great knowledge of Islamic philosophy and literature, a sense of community of spirit with all men of goodwill. 'Islam at its best and truest wins the recognition of everyman's commonsense. It speaks of the sovereignty of God and the brotherhood of men, and of Taw'hid—harmony—the great unifying principle underlying art and science and morality itself.'

My host confessed to being somewhat lonely and isolated within the household of his faith precisely because of his readiness for self-criticism and openness to others. He pointed to the failures of contemporary Islam. Things that his society professed with one voice and denied with the other. 'Islam was originally not a tyrannical prescription for reaction, but a programme of social action, which could still offer a real alternative to communism and to capitalism. What you see in many of today's Muslim nations, so-called, is the betrayal of Islam.' His critique of contemporary Islam went far to make his faith attractive and compelling. He wasn't presenting a front. He was laying bare a remarkable soul. 'We have so much to teach each other, so much in common. I need to understand, to feel within me your Christian awareness of suffering in love. You need to recognise as deeply the Muslim instinct for grappling with the realities of responsibility and power.' But it was his last sentence which brought us nearest, and yet left us in the end, I felt, furthest apart. 'Together we share the precious understanding of a personal God, a personal communion with God. I covet this more and more for both of us.'

Five pillars

In an English industrial city, a group of Christians gathered in a friend's house, meeting to try to learn about Islam. The two Muslim spokesmen offered the greatest imaginable contrast. Dr A., a reticent man with a reputation for tremendous pastoral concern for fellow-Muslims, and indeed for all his patients, was tall, thin, grey-haired, hesitant. Mr K., a lawyer, vehement, politically active, chairman of various committees, was short, broad, voluble. He very soon launched into his basic theme. Islam was the way for modern man. He began with a salutary attack on the spiritual and moral bankruptcy of the Western world, the blame for which he placed firmly at the door of Christianity. The false spiritualising and individualism of Christianity, its morbid preoccupation with sin and suffering, its pessimistic view of man, its narrow asceticism, were presented as the source of its fundamental social ineffectiveness.

Islam, on the other hand, he asserted, was now the great remedy for our condition. It restored the proper relationship of spirit to matter, of law to freedom, of individual to community, of private ownership to common weal. Islam was ever a faith in action, a revelation of truth but also a social order. The five pillars on which modern life must be reconstructed are plain. They bring about a just social order without the racial and economic discrimination so typical of Christianity. Faith, Prayer, Fasting, Charity and Pilgrimage provide these simple foundations.

Mr K. wanted us to return to the intense combustion point of Muhammad's original vision. First in the Qur'an, and then out of the great centuries of expansion and consolidation, the laws and traditions were hammered out in the heat of conflict and conquest. Now Mr K. sought, like many modern revival movements in Islam, to recapture the original thrust and fervour: Islam, powered by its new God-given wealth and political ascendancy, has the dynamic which could reorganise societies and nations on the supreme foundation of God's sovereign, all-comprehending will.

Finally, he reminded us that Europe derived much of the foundation of its cultural development from the rich source of Islamic civilisation of the eighth to the twelfth centuries. The new emphasis on culture by modern Muslims was a vital reassertion of their own dignity and value in the face of European pretensions. But even more—the harmonies, the poise of free-flowing invention and overall control in a mosque or a miniature, a colonnade or the detail of an inlaid pencase were themselves celebrations of Taw'hid, harmony, the creative order, the 'rope of God', the all-controlling purpose and design for lack of which modern man is perishing.

Hidden doors
Dr A. had been shifting in his chair. Suddenly he cleared his throat, and said softly: 'But is this ... this outward material triumph, the thing to present of Islam? Surely that is just where Christianity went wrong in the last centuries? It was not too spiritual, as you suggest. Rather it was too materialistic. But I believe there is another,

hidden way which true believers of all faiths find. It is the way to which the Prophet points us, to which God calls those whom he would make his 'friends' in every age. If you would go by this path, look more deeply into your Scriptures, my Christian friends, and then study ours. Look at the life of the Prophet, the Tradition, the lives of our saints, and you will find it is all the same. There have been so many who were drawn to this path from the beginning. There are stories of them, collections of their prayers, men who prepared themselves day and night for everlasting life with God, men for whom earth seemed to slip away under their feet and the Mecca, the dawning of true light, opened up. They walk by obedience and faith, meditating on the Qur'an and discovering its inner meaning. They pass through a whole series of states of feeling, and of conditions of soul, stages on the spiritual journey. Even in this life we can catch sight of immortality. We can at least begin to pass away from self and to become one with God.

'I would like to call you to share with me and all other true seekers in this inward quest. As the Qur'an says: "If my servant enquire of me, lo I am near, yes, nearer to a man than his own jugular vein.... Whithersoever you turn, there is the face of God."' Dr A.'s very face was shining. Mr K. looked a bit unhappy. 'Our main task is to discover in this life already what is said in the Qur'an of the blessed in paradise: "He loveth them and they love him." God in his mercy takes this first step towards man to draw him to him with the cords of love. "My Earth and my Heaven contain me not, but the heart of my faithful servant containeth me."'

Dr A. was now thoroughly warmed. He launched into a long series of stories of men of God and their sayings through the centuries, and then of quotations from mystics and poets on the theme of the Divine Love in which God and man are one. This, he suggested, was the true Taw'hid. (At this, poor Mr K. was shaking his head and grasping his brow and muttering 'This is not Islam'.) Finally, Dr A. quoted the wonderful phrases of the prayer manuals, like those of a famous night-prayer said to be spoken on a roof-top under the sky.

My God and my Lord, eyes are at rest, stars are setting, hushed are the movements of birds in their nests, of monsters in the deep. And Thou art the Just who knowest no change, the Equity that swerveth not, the Everlasting that passeth not away. The doors of kings are locked, watched by their bodyguards; but Thy door is open to him who calls on Thee. My Lord, each lover is now alone with his beloved, and Thou art for me the Beloved!

Back streets

I was next to hear the words of that prayer in a very different place. A social worker friend took me to tea with Fatima, a widow in a little red-brick Midland street. There, in the polished front room, were framed Qur'anic writings and pictures of the Kaba'a, the holy stone of Mecca. A smell of joss sticks came from the small room behind, where Fatima's youngest son was ill. She was worried about him and was in search of remedies. Back home she would have taken him to the shrine of a local saint. Even now she had a tenuous link with the lost comfort of that shrine with its nocturnal drummings and chantings, its little lights and throng of suppliants: Karim, the little boy, had tied round his wrist for protection a piece of cloth brought back from one of the festivals by a kind friend. In exchange, a thread had been tied to the saint's tomb and money put in a box there. Poor Karim had other adornments. On his arm was another band of cloth with a small booklet, a tiny Qur'an in a pocket to ward off evil spirits.

She had many troubles. Anees, her eldest son, apprentice at a factory, was a faithful boy, but she was more anxious for Kassim, the other boy, and for Tasneem, rebellious daughter torn between the pop-fan world of her school friends and the irksome restraints of home. 'Pray for them,' she said. She showed me the little prayer manuals she had brought from home. Fatima explained that she loved to use the Bismillah, the formula 'In the Name of God, the Merciful, the Compassionate'. 'It is very great power,' she said. 'But there is power in all the Names of God, is that not so? That's why I pray "Grant me a Name from your Names of Light." And there's a hidden Name, a great, unknown Name.' Later she came back to this. 'Show me how you pray. Would you pray for Karim? I have heard that the Name of Jesus is powerful—is it so?'

Across the gap
The question brought me back to my many talks with Thomas, another Indian from the same area originally. He was from his birth something of a pilgrim. His parents' death made that break from the traditional community that a man may need in this life if he is to find his way freely. It left him with an inner gap, a loneliness, an emptiness over which life seemed suspended. He was driven on in his hunger and thirst for truth. He became versed in the intricacies of the law. He also studied the first philosophers of Islam. He met one of the more sophisticated thinkers practising dialogue with the modern Western world and felt the sharpness of the questions raised. Still he was hungry.

He drifted to Baghdad and worked for a welfare organisation for pilgrims coming to visit the vast ornate silver- and gold-plated shrines, tombs of Imams, the great Muslim religious teachers. From Indonesia, Malaysia, Kenya, India and Pakistan they came. Many were the long conversations he had in the great community of the faithful.

Gradually the quest drew him towards the daunting wasteland of Europe. Eventually he became a social worker and joined the staff of a study centre linked with Mr K., but also took time to read in the mystical writings beloved of Dr A., which stirred him strangely. It was then that he met the friendship and open, accepting hospitality of an English family, who seemed deeply interested in him and his faith. 'I had seen the grandeur and the majesty of God in Hyderabad, in Delhi, in Damascus. I had felt him outside me and shared the shadowy longings of men for him. But he never came *inside* my own soul, with my own self. I couldn't take him into myself as a person. I couldn't see how I could matter in this great vastness.'

Out of his words came a sudden flash of that richly figured ornamentation, so frequent in Islamic art, as a kind of filigree screen, a pattern over a void, 'moving upon silence'. In that art there is always a consciousness of a transcendent abyss. It was as if Thomas saw the passionately worked intricacies of the moral and legal structure as it sprang molten from the Prophet's vision, and the later expansion, the brilliant displays of rationality in the theorising of the Muslim philosphers, the heaped images, the states and stages of mystics, the detailed prescriptions of rituals, the precise formalisations, the multiplications of names and formulae, of intentions and blessings, as a kind of play upon emptiness. The gulf at the centre of the Prophet's sightings had never been truly filled.

And it seemed as if into this very void the loving words and actions of his friends slipped gradually into place. The miracle was realised. There came the conceiving and embodying of the eternal in a form that reached him and grasped him finally—God with us, God with him at last in the only possible fully personal form of the living, dying, broken and reintegrated Christ.

Recommended books

Alfred Guillaume, *Islam* (Pelican Books, 1969). Perhaps still the clearest short introduction to Islam.

Fazlur Rahman, *Islam* (Weidenfeld & Nicolson, 1966). Fine outline picture of Islam from a critical Muslim scholar.

Khurshid Ahmad (ed.), *Islam—its meaning and message* (Islamic Council of Europe, 1975). An official Muslim viewpoint.

Constance Padwick, *Muslim Devotions* (SPCK, 1961). A rich treasury of Muslim prayer.

A. J. Arberry, *Sufism* (Allen & Unwin, 1950). Sufi mysticism.

J. Schacht and C. E. Bosworth, *The Legacy of Islam* (OUP, new edition, 1974). Muslim culture.
D. Talbot Rice, *Islamic Art* (Thames & Hudson, 1975).

Response to Islam
II: Broken Circles

The 'World of Islam' festival which took place in London, back in 1976, was a pointer both to the rise of new economic and political powers in the world and to the emergence of Islam as the second largest religion in Europe. The organisers of the Festival disclaimed any political purpose and declared their intention as purely educational, although they acknowledged financial support from Islamic governments.

Crossing the threshold
The Festival, a series of exhibitions, televised films and concerts laid on with the help of scholars, museums, the BBC and others, came as a reminder that we are surrounded everywhere today by the entrances to other people's worlds and opportunities to explore. We continually stand at this particular threshold, with various attractive forces inviting us to cross. Not only was there the attraction of the theme, the beauty and quality of the exhibits gleaming within, the reminder of the immense creative contribution of Islam to human civilisation—including our own. There was also the obvious desire of the sponsors to bring at the very least their culture to our attention and to dispel what they felt to be the ignorance and the distorted impressions of Islam which have prevailed among us.

Behind us, also urging us to enter, are the voices and experiences of that great line of westerners who have pioneered the way into this fascinating territory before us. For members and friends of CMS this line includes in particular a succession of missionaries from Henry Martyn to the great Temple Gairdner and beyond. In latter years we hear the voices of Max Warren with his 'theology of attention' urging us to look and listen, of Bishop David Brown in his 'Guidelines' document, and supremely of Bishop Kenneth Cragg whose great *Call of the Minaret* hears the high, piercing summons of the Muezzin as an appeal to Christians also for understanding, for service, and for patient meeting. These and countless others concerned for the household of Islam point to the way in. They urge us to inform ourselves, to read, to study.

Above all we are being given the opportunity for relationships with Muslims. This should be the kind of honest, perceptive and sensitive friendship, through which illusions are dispelled, confidences are shared and within which alone a new knowledge of Christ can ever be communicated.

Religions—the real change

After we really set foot across the threshold, we shall be on our way to an eventual and slowly realised understanding of what new knowledge of Christ might mean. Only from deep within the relationship that is offered us will we even begin to discern a new shape for the Gospel itself. But first you simply open your mind and imagination wide to enjoy the record of 1,300 years of artistic and intellectual activity. The vital calligraphy over and around all, the poignantly vivid clarity of the miniatures, the ceramics, the magnificent woven stuffs, the brocades and the silks, the elaboration of glass and jewellery, the play of patternings on carpets ranging from the softest, most naturalistic flowers on a green ground, to the severest geometry.... It brings to mind successive cities, like present-day Isfahan, ringing with craftsmen's hammers, humming with looms, source of a seemingly endless range of unity in diversity.

And this is the aspect of it all which begins to take hold

of you—the astonishing coherence of this whole, fantastic, figured spread in time and space that is the phenomenon of Islam. Gradually it bears in upon you 'the way in which a completely definite style, a whole repertory of motifs and an architectural system became, quite early in the Hegira (Muhammad's migration from Mecca to Medina), associated with an idea and a faith' (David Talbot Rice), 'the power of dogma ... over form and creation' (Kenneth Cragg). 'Within Islam,' said the Festival brochure 'culture (*adab*) embraces all the sciences, physical, philosophical and philological. All knowledge is interrelated and interlocking and its understanding is made possible by the revelations of God's purpose to Mankind.'

Of course you could say something similar about Byzantine Christendom and the whole legacy of Constantine and Theodosius. Perhaps this is partly why it was so easily possible for a Christian basilica to turn into a mosque like Santa Sofia, or for a mosque to turn again into a basilica like Cordoba after the Christian conquest. But this sense of a total system was never entirely central to the Christian gospel. The spirit always stirred uneasily at its heart—it was churchianity, an acquired triumphal mode —whereas for Islam this is of the essence. As Dr Cragg puts it, 'Muhammad was from the outset its Constantine as well as its prophet.' The original and fundamental contrast is between Jesus, whose kingdom is not of this age, setting his face to go up to Jerusalem and the Cross, and Muhammad, at his crucial moment, setting out on the Hegira to establish his temporal power at Medina. For him, as for Constantine, the Divine will is confirmed by his conquest and his very material success. The Qur'an could not allow the Cross even to Jesus himself. It firmly established a theocracy in which the will of obedient man becomes harmoniously continuous with the revealed will of God. Heaven could be well nigh realised upon earth.

Traditional religious systems frequently give an impression of this kind of totality. It is not surprising, perhaps, that Wilfred Cantwell Smith and John Hick seem to look at all religions as if they were a series of equivalent overlapping systems wheeling around a central abstract transcendent divinity. Then comes John Hick's claim about the modern Copernican revolution in which we all suddenly discover that our own system is only partial, that each system is valid for its own society, that each can learn from the other and that not Christ nor the Qur'an nor the Ancestors are at the centre but the impersonal unity they all reflect.

Towards a fully personal God

The true picture seems to me to be very different. A real Copernican revolution certainly comes about wherever we discover, as many Christians have been compelled to and Muslims are just beginning to, that the unified system itself must be an illusion. The great circle of Heaven and Earth has always been broken not only by our creatureliness, but also by the tragic fact of evil and sin, the 'not yet' of the New Testament. It will be a reality beyond this life. Meanwhile we can have only transient experiences of wholeness.

It is the possibility of that ultimate completion to which Christ broke through on his Cross—the Cross which to the mystic theosophist is foolishness and to the moralist and legalist a stumbling block. And to that Cross all religious systems, like all individual natures, all creatures, all societies and cultures, must come to be broken and turned round. We must all needs come to this only place of forgiveness, of healing and reintegration, pass through this death and this resurrection to our fulfilment. Christendom and many Christianities again and again must be broken here. So also Islam, Hinduism, Humanism, any other of the circles, have to come to this judgment and this mercy seat at which God has appointed, as St Paul put it to the Athenians, the world should be judged (the often neglected climax to that particular sermon).

The revolution is simply the discovery by a new secularism of this crisis for all culture and all religion. A student in a Muslim country can assure a western visitor that this breach in the unity of culture 'can't happen here'.

But in fact everywhere it is coming or it has come. As a missionary in a Muslim country writes,

> I asked a young Muslim only yesterday what the word *jaid*, usually translated ignorance, meant. He said it means a man who knows nothing of civilisation. Ten years ago his reply would have been 'knows nothing of religion'.

A swing from religion to culture as the basis for Islam is coming in many places. All societies must pass through this particular 'fiery brook' in which the traditional framework melts and disintegrates.

What then do we find after this breakup? What remains to us? First we begin to discover as we grope about in the ruins the gradual emergence of a sense of *common humanity*, of common human needs and dangers, of our universal predicament on this threatened planet. It is to this kind of theme that the World Council of Churches has directed its specially sponsored discussions between men of different faiths in recent years.

Even more deeply, as the regulating and organising structures of the world of faith crumble and fall away, we are suddenly made more aware of the naked human yearnings, questionings and struggles of ordinary people the world over. Supremely we discover a whole community of quests in our prayers. Anthologies like Constance Padwick's *Muslim Devotions* or Kenneth Cragg's *Alive Unto God* show so many of the same creaturely responses, the same hopes and joys, the same longing for forgiveness whereby men and women everywhere all unbeknown fling themselves at the foot of the same cross.

These yearnings all coalesce around the search of people moving out of traditional societies, extended families, village communities, into a bewildering mass world. It is a search for the *personal*, for a new way of feeling and being, a freely chosen corporate existence which can transcend and fulfil the former way of being. Perhaps this is the heart of the real Copernican change in society that accompanies secularism. And surely this fundamental movement will find its final direction only when it begins to touch upon the possibility of the truly personal God towards whom history itself ultimately moves. For this discovery every moment of breakup and crisis becomes the moment of opportunity. As we feel our way through the ruins we can yet come to discover alongside us, so to speak, One who amid the glittering fragments of our false unities walks with us, faces with us the broken circle, the chaos, the disillusionment, the abyss. He tenderly reinforces our hopes and joys, heals our sadness and releases within and among us a truly personal grace, God with us. It is here that the Muezzin's cry, the Prophet's vision, the convictingly humble obeisances of rhythmic devotion of the faithful will be fulfilled in the end.

Because only an embodied and suffering God can be a fully personal God. And only a fully personal God can adequately meet the needs and aspirations of men and women. Beyond the archaeological beauty he stands sole in the end, grasping us each in his sovereign love, the only One who can draw us on through the dissolution of our earthly patternings into his resurrection.

Depth of friendship
But to come this far, we have got to go out and meet Muslims. We have got to move among them, some of us where and when possible to live among them. We have to learn languages, not only literally at times, but also metaphorically—the language of their symbols, their customs, their devotions, their whole rhythm of life. Christ comes alive between us in such a variety of ways, as much in absences, in contrasts as in alleged parallels. The vital connecting places vary in different contexts. They seem to come about often in the discussion of prayer and of how we pray. In Northern Nigeria the Qur'anic teachings about Jesus, the Messiah, the word of God, born of the Spirit, given power more than any other man (even Muhammad) to give sight to the blind, to heal lepers and to raise the dead to life, has offered a way to fuller faith confessed

suddenly in the wondering words of a Hausa with a newly
dawning conviction, 'Yes, truly he is the Saviour of the
world.'

The desperate need is that the loss of the old habits of
life should not leave a mere void. When one of the most
integrally unified, harmonious orderings of life that ever
sought to house the human soul falls apart, what then?
That is the question which haunts the magnificence of the
World of Islam Festival.

The answer may lie in unlikely places. A missionary in a
Muslim country in Africa together with an inspired local
worker is doing a great deal to change the fearful, ignorant
or contemptuous attitudes of apathetic church members,
partly by role play and mime, partly by discussion. Then as
they venture out into friendship with Muslims they
discover points of common interest and need. In
discussions among Muslim women they find that it is in
talk about their worries, their temptations, their battles
with Satan, their yearning for forgiveness, their fears
about local events, that, as the Christian worker puts it,
'we walk along the road of life together until we come to
the corner'. Among those Christians who work in an equal
relationship with Muslims as teachers or nurses, questions
about the job, secular education, the death of a baby, the
treatment of another person, all lead into the heart of much
greater questionings, and give opportunity for a witness
which is also a freely invited and loving response.

For all such opportunities we have to wait until they
come and it may mean a lifetime of quiet sympathy and
service in the background. It is bound to mean very costly
patience, long-suffering and humility.

When Bishop Hassan Dehqani-Tafti of Iran, one of the
most perceptive and imaginative of those seeking to draw
Islam into a new and fulfilling relationship with Christ
today, went to his Muslim father's funeral, his brothers
debated furiously whether there could be any place for him
in the mosque. At length moderation just prevailed and he
was conceded a position at the back, among the shoes of
the worshippers and near to the poorest. It was not

difficult, he said, to overcome his pride and take up his place there. After all it proved to be a joy to stand at the 'lowest place' greeting and ushering others to a 'higher place', 'because this is the very thing,' as he wrote, 'I have been called to do in my life. Christianity has always talked to Islam from a domineering and superior position. No wonder they regard us as unclean! There is nothing so unclean and disgusting as pride and domination. If we want to have a dialogue with Islam we must be ready to stand at the lowest place greeting them. ... At the end of the service the objectors including the Chief Mullah accompanied me into the house and were most gracious.' As he drove back he thought over again the sight of that tough and enduring little congregation of villagers. 'I could not help feeling their tremendous need to know the real heart of God. I knew this would not happen unless the Church is ready to sit with them, but at the lowest place.'

Recommended books

M. M. Pickthall, *The meaning of the Glorious Qur'an* (Mentor Books, 1954). An explanatory version of the Qur'an in English

Kenneth Cragg (ed.), *Alive to God* (OUP, 1970). Muslim prayer
Constance Padwick, *Muslim Devotions* (SPCK, 1961). Muslin prayer

Kenneth Cragg, *The Call of the Minaret* (OUP, 1956). The Christian approach to Islam
David Brown, *A New Threshold*, Guidelines for the Churches in their relations with Muslim communities (British Council of Churches, 1976).
David Brown, *Doorways and Doorsteps* (CMS Annual Sermon, 1975). The Christian approach to Islam

General books on other faiths and inter-faith dialogues including reference to Islam:
David Brown (ed.) *A Guide to Religions* (T.E.F. Study Guide No. 12, SPCK, 1975). Chapter on Islam and concluding chapter by David Brown.

Norman Anderson, *The World's Religions* (Inter-Varsity Press, 1953). Chapter on Islam and concluding chapter by Norman Anderson.
John Stott, *Christian Mission in the Modern World* (Falcon, 1975). Especially chapter on dialogue.

Audio-visual aid
The Way of Islam, a filmstrip with open-reel tape or cassette commentary (CMS, 1975).

A Faith in Travail

A friend's impression of an oil city in the Arabian Gulf stirred vivid memories. I could see the desert mirage, the eruption of tower blocks in the shimmering haze, unbelievable strips of bright green watered grass, the vast construction site. All the contradictions of that city made up of layers of immigrants—European, Asian, African— living cut off from each other and the scattering of their white-robed Arab hosts. A confused and divided world, founded on a brief frenzied scramble for wealth.

Starting place
But somewhere in the centre I recalled one building in particular. Not the ostentatious crowded mosque, but a little old fort-like palace. It had the impoverished dignity of a former ruler, deposed because he preferred 'a handful of dates' to the incomprehensible lure of progress. He had wanted to stick to his little settlement of fishermen, traders and pearl-divers.

The free, fierce, open-handed rule of such men seemed to point back beyond their narrow creed to an earlier, larger age. First the simple word of the Prophet remade Medina and Mecca. Then, as a new source of unity, the basic Qur'anic commands, humane, egalitarian, imbued with an awareness of a righteous, personal God, carried a widening empire far out over the decayed complexity of the late Byzantine world by the sheer force of their moral power and coherence. They were expanded to embrace various new or inherited cultures without losing their consistency.

Dr Hedayatullah, a Muslim commentator, points out

that Muslims of that era were secure enough in the cohesiveness of their faith to be strikingly open to others. They enlarged and adapted the growing collection of oral 'traditions' of the Prophet to supplement the Qur'an. They developed a huge body of law, the famous *Sharia*, to include many institutions and rituals that are now part of Islam, but which have no actual basis in the Qur'an. Islamic empires remained, like their Roman and Hellenistic predecessors, relatively tolerant, pluralist societies in which different religious communities could co-exist peacefully.

Only in the days of decline and recession under the pressure of seventeenth- and eighteenth-century European powers, claims Dr Hedayatullah, did the shutters come down, and a new defensive rigidity close in. It was then for the most part that women were veiled, and shut away—a sharp contrast with the scope and dignity afforded them in the Qur'an. The authority of narrow-minded, fatalistic 'scribes' (*ulama*) was strengthened.

Scattered caravan

This was the start of a long process in which, as Kalim Siddiqui puts it, the Muslim caravan was 'blown off course and dispersed by the ravages of history ...' That dispersion was doubly traumatic.

First was the desolating wound of the gradual subjugation of Islamic areas over two centuries by the western powers, until by the end of the first world war hardly any Islamic country was free from some kind of dominance. 'For 200 years we suffered an incomprehensible fate at the hands of non-Muslims ...' It seemed a contradiction in terms, an intolerable offence still deeply and confusedly felt by many in a way which they have not yet been able to come to terms with. After all, nothing in their history or theology could have prepared them for this shock. They had had few experiences of being a subject people. Their whole tradition had been true to the Prophet's own conviction that his call was to be confirmed by conquest.

Second, through this wound of outward defeat, there entered in a far more penetrating and irreversible agent of inner change: western institutions, western education, science and philosophy, western secularism. For the first time what had become a closed world was forced to pass through the 'fiery brook' of western relativism. All cultures have had to pass through it, or will have to do so, into the new secularised world of modern technology. The old religious frameworks are breaking up, for good as well as for ill.

Since the renaissance, Westerners have had time, at least to some extent, to grow accustomed to successive waves of secularism, to an extended process of rational criticism and scientific enquiry, to the notion of secular government. Westerners may see toleration as having profoundly Christian roots in the whole radical non-conformist tradition. For many Muslims such changes in values and social patterns are deeply disorientating. And the pain and bewilderment have been compounded by the way in which such changes first made their appearance, seemingly imposed by conquest.

Attempts to reform
Few such emotions troubled the first liberal-minded westernising politicians who took the helm of their newly independent countries in the 1950s. Leaders such as Nasser, following the example of Kemal Ataturk in the 20s, pushed through a modernising drive with scant regard for fundamentalist Muslim groups or the waning power of the old religious authorities, and took most of the new generation with them.

But from the 60s on the reaction came. It was made up of a two-fold disillusionment. Bewilderment at the disruptive effect of so much bureaucracy, an unheaval in which people swithered between traditional values and uncertain new expectations. But also frustration at the widening gap between rich and poor, epitomised by Cairo itself, the failure of the vaunted fruits of modernisation to trickle downwards, a mounting resentment of the permissive ways of the élite and the inequalities of the consumer society with its gross dependence on the West.

There has been all over the Muslim world in recent years a mounting nostalgic reaction against western materialism, a kind of agonised cry of 'close the universe again', a sharp rejection of the 'open doors' of all would-be progressives.

In every Muslim country there has been a popular resurgence of reactionary groups from the *da'wah* (missionary) movements of Malaysia, urging the casting out of radios and TV sets and the burning of furniture, inspiring student girls to veil themselves and 'drop out' from college, to the 'Society for Repentance and Flight from the World', in Egypt, to whose leader even Saudi Arabia is heretically and sinfully modern.

At the same time widespread campaigns for the thorough-going restoration of the traditional Shariat law have attracted votes and influenced courts of justice and government leaders, always sensitive to such shifts in public opinion. In Malaysia and Iran and elsewhere trivial examples of sexual licence—physical proximity or public kissing—have been loudly condemned and heavily punished.

And yet the oil wealth which has powered the resurgence of Islam has at the same time been eating away at its heart. The huge inrush of westernised expatriates continually brings in a new life-style, new tastes, new expectations. The mass of immigrant labourers—Pathan, Baluchi, North Yemeni—export the same kinds of change, together with inflation in the wage packets they send home. Countries receiving 'oil aid' have their own troubled economies and shifting cultures distorted.

Perhaps the greatest pathos is to be found not in sporadic spontaneous popular movements, cries of pain out of the general confusion, but in the concerted official attempt of the oil powers to cast out the sickness that consumes them. This has taken the form of a succession of Islamic world conferences, beginning as far back as 1926. The 70s saw the most grandiose series ever, for the most part hosted by Saudi Arabia, though Colonel Gaddafi made an unsuccessful bid for the initiative at a youth gathering in Tripoli in 1973. And there was the great assembly in London's Royal Albert Hall in 1976.

At all of these there have been the same bursts of often aggressive rhetoric, the same flurry of high expectancy, proceedings conducted with pomp and verve. Institutions have been founded, like the Islamic Foundation in Leicester; a network of vigorous propagandist bodies has been set in motion, like the Islamic Council for Europe. Apologists talk of great programmes of research and of grand strategy. Experts in every field are invoked.

At the heart of it lies always a sharp repudiation of the West that has its roots in a long struggle. The West, say many voices, has entered our bones and veins and has undervalued us. We cannot forgive our conquerors for having betrayed us into this strange social landscape of the twentieth century, all our landmarks gone.

There is a fierce repudiation of Christian missions, seen as deceptively and exploitingly abusing education, medicine, aid. The Chambesy discussion between Christians and Muslims reported in *The International Review of Mission* for October 1976 so harshly disclosed this hostility that on the Christian side Bishop Kenneth Cragg after a lifetime spent in such dialogue confessed himself 'desolated' by the tone of the argument. Christianity is still to many Muslim spokesmen an ineffective dualistic religion which, by separating the spiritual and material, by its irresponsible mysticism and its individualism, has lost control of its own society, let alone anyone else's.

Now, Muslims say, there is need for a new basis for humanity, a new structure for civilisation, a Qur'anic critique brought to bear on economics, social sciences, philosophy, providing a new foundation for modern thought. New Muslim intellectuals must replace the old religious leaders (*ulama*). An effort must be made to restore 'an elightened theocracy', a new economic and social order with an Islamic hierarchy of values. This is admitted to be a 'gigantic task'. But it is the only way in which to found a stable, ordered, united society, the integrated life for man which Islam, his true saviour, must now provide.

It all sounds impressive, but in the end, what can it really amount to? Behind all the arguments lurks the inevitable ultimate recognition that no distinctive *Islamic* science or solution is really likely to emerge, only surely in the end a good human solution to our problems which Muslims, Christians and those of all other faiths or of none *may* find if they work together. The Muslim economic prescriptions still basically add up to Kalim Siddiqui's summary of the situation at Tripoli 'communism plus Allah or capitalism minus interest', which latter no Islamic country dreams in reality of practising.

Meeting point
Christians who have faced such a crisis of faith should be the first to sympathise with all this. Alas, so many of us are still bewildered and defensive, and hence aggressive to other faiths. But if the old worlds are broken, the old arrogances cast down, and we are all minorities now, then what will ever be gained by fierce counter moves? Fear and hardness must be cast out, a very hard lesson for minority Churches in Muslim lands to accept. It is so hard to trust God to be enough, and to be vulnerable, when you are really up against it in a way that western Christians are not. And yet the New Testament gives us the model.

The only answer is humble, honest, penitent compassion, the *suffering with* Muslims, and others too, which the Cross makes possible. Ramon Lull saw long ago—as Max Warren would point out to us—that there was no room in Christ for any other way. Lull, who had been himself a hard-liner, ultimately recognised that that way must be 'by love, by prayer, by tears and the offering up of lives'.

It is not surprising that we find numbers of perceptive, sensitive Muslims coming to meet us. They have seen the truth that in the breaking and stripping away of all institutional frameworks, naked searching human beings will find God afresh not through hard assertion but only through facing pain.

Muhammed Talbi of Tunisia maintains that Islam must face man's agonised self-questioning. The Egyptian writer Kemal Hussein, in his *City of Wrong*, begins to accept a kind of necessity for the Cross. Professor Hasan Askari, a Muslim scholar, takes this further as he sees that Islam has failed to come to terms with the last two centuries of its history. In search of a critique of its triumphalism he has told how he 'turned to the Christian consciousness and there discovered that the Islamic consciousness needs, *in its own framework, of course*, the category of the Cross' (italics mine).

God is only God, truly and fully personal, when he meets us not in some grand design, but in our failure to achieve any design. On the Cross he bears our brokenness and incompleteness and meets us in our confusion. Only in that meeting is the final 'Islam', the real submission, made possible at last for us all: only then can we begin to envisage the birth of a world restored.

Recommended reading

Fazlur Rahman, *Islam* (Weidenfeld & Nicolson, 1966). Sensitive, honest and searching account of Islam's historical development.
Khursid Ahmad (ed.), *Islam, its meaning and message* (Islamic Council of Europe, 1975). An expression of the more 'revivalist' approach referred to above.
Kalim Siddiqui, *Towards a new destiny* (The Open Press, 1974). A subtler comment, raising more of the questions.
Clifford Geertz, *Islam Observed* (University of Chicago Press, 1971). A social anthropologist's stimulating account of Islam's response to secularism in two situations.

The Dream is Over

In the early 60s Cambridge presented to a returning traveller a transformed scene. A survivor from the 50s could feel like a Rip van Winkle waking into a new college. The same court, but what very different faces looking disenchantedly out of the gothic windows! The sudden abundance of hair, the frayed jeans, the beat of the background music, showed the students suddenly bound up together with the window cleaners on their ladders outside, following faintly pursuing the new movement spreading from the States via Merseyside. Adolescents suddenly had the ball at their feet. Fed on demand from the outset, given a special significance, theirs was the first generation to grow up alongside that flickering stream of fact and fantasy which is television, with its looming and fading faces and moods. They were the first wave of the products of a long-hidden social revolution, undinted by military service, strengthened by the new purchasing power which economic growth had put into their hands, ready to make their impact felt.

Great expectations
With a sudden spasm of twentieth-century romanticism, a new unity and community were expected to spring into being on a basis of feeling and intuition set over against rationality; freedom against inhibiting control; loose clothes and shagginess against definitions and categories; spontaneity against planning; sexuality and mystical oneness with everything against the discontinuities and restrictions of industrialised life. On a surging rush of

ear-battering chords, part tantrum, part confused yearning, all a sensuous, gut-stirring black-influenced sound, the 'Now' generation, as they were to call themselves, had taken off in the late 50s on their apocalyptic quest for an instant new heaven and earth. The *shamans* of early rock and their successors the prophets, Titanic heroes, visionaries of the 60s, became cult leaders and endowed with almost messianic significance. Bob Dylan, frail figure 'as if on a death trip', slender and drawn, became the bearer of the hopes, fears and the projection of his followers. The Beatles, with their magical vitality, had epileptics and cripples pushed at them for healing 'as if something could rub off' them.

The early 60s protest phase saw Bob Dylan moving into the centre of a movement made up of a whole range of idealistic groups, old and new left, students, teenagers, and articulating the mood of the moment in songs such as *Blowin' in the Wind* and later *The times they are a changin'*. He reapplied the romantically revived folk tradition to the issues of his time in a skilful pastiche. It wasn't a genuine folk product any more than Dylan was a genuine 'hobo'. So much in the new movement was bogus as its stars, the chief victims, knew well. Dylan's real name was Zimmermann and he was escaping like so many of his fans from a small-town background into this fantasy of a lonely folk poet out of nowhere. A performer was forced to become a personality before he could become a person. The commercial system in the shape of 'the cats with the big cigars' of Tin Pan Alley closed in on the folk protest movement and undermined it with imitation and promotion as they had done to the early rock movement before it. Disillusionment set in. Dylan began to question the naîve assumptions they had all been making. He seemed to sense a falsity in the emotion generated and in his own self-projection. Even in opposing the system he was part of it. Politics were unreal:

No one's free
Even the birds are chained to the sky.

The Beatles and other groups had not long swept in with a fresh burst of original revitalised rock. Under their influence he started to give his folk songs more of a rock backing. Then, together, they moved into a second phase of marijuana and mysticism.

The journey of the decade turned inwards. External form and function were repudiated. What was needed was a 'change of consciousness'. Marcuse's blend of Marx and Freud wanting to remove all repressive institutions so that the new society could burst into flower, Leary's philosophy of drugs, Ginsberg's mysticism and the I Ching merged with a new surrealism, parables, psychedelic symbols. 'Rimbaud's where it's at.' The singers became seers harking back to the romantic French symbolist poets of the nineteenth century, Rimbaud and Baudelaire, making bright images of transcendence to illuminate the shadowy horrors of modern life, breaking out of the cultural hang-ups of the authoritarians, writing 'from inside them' and setting it to the visceral beat of 'electricity like a squadron of jet planes'. Dylan was poet of the juke boxes, chanting his revelation in taut, nasal tones. But commercialisation destroyed this phase too and the new illusion of being genuine at last. For Dylan as for Lennon this too became just 'freaky psychedelic claptrap', the instant mysticism dissolved, another set of feelings was burnt out.

Aftermath

The Beatles broke up. Bob Dylan had his car crash and used it as an excuse to flee and hide. They fade from view into the 'morning after' with its flashbacks and air of *déja vu*. 'The media feed the illusion and will eventually destroy it all', as John Lennon puts it. Both he and Bob Dylan's biographer echo a phrase from the first disillusionment at the end of the protest era—'The dream is over'. For Lennon 'it's the same game, nothing's really changed. . . . It's just that a lot of people have long hair, that's all'. He gives a devastating critique of the tours, the publicity, the phoniness of it all. Nothing is left. 'Beatles is the final thing I no longer believe in because I no longer believe in myth and Beatles is another myth. I'm talking about the generation thing. The dream is over. It's over and gotta, well, I have anyway personally get down to so-called reality.' For Lennon this means, in a frequent post-sixties words, 'survival'. Day to day 'that's what it's all about, just cherishing each day and dreading it too. . . . Hold on. There's nothing else to do'.

In a sense, for all the rapid turnover of new sound and names and scenes, the 70s were bound to remain, in this area, something of an aftermath. The jeans and the long hair had become a habit, a convention. The idea of a separate style for the young had come to stay, the casualness, the informal directness, the fundamental questioning of our society, the championing of the oppressed, the belief in participation, these are widely accepted themes. The language of universal love of the late 60s is still used, though it has rather lost its force. But there isn't really a coherent youth culture any more. There are those, many in their forties, still on the hippie trail, still in communes. Pop festivals have become a predictable routine. There's been more of a turning from drugs to alcohol. But, as with sex for its own sake, as with mysticism or yoga taken up rapidly and superficially, young people tend to become disillusioned earlier with such sensation. Pop music widely diversified is no longer so much a group thing as a matter of individual taste. It has become massively commercialised and institutionalised. There are flashes of creativity as with the increasing ethnic music through which different cultures are finding a wider audience. There's the angry sound of reggae, of the new West Indian generation voicing their pain. But otherwise it's all much of a collage of fragments of the 60s. Heavy hard rock, the favourite, the more nostalgic tranquillised soft rock, or middle rock, source of the wallpaper music background noise on which our culture has come to depend. There is even, for the teenyboppers, youngsters' music so that, like an embryo, they can have gone through—in every sense—all the experiences of their immediate elders by the time they come to adult birth.

Three phases
Past figures still over-shadow the varied gyrations of today's mosaic. Dylan was accused by his fans of deserting them like the French poet Rimbaud, who turned to the safety of a merchant's life. In fact he would seem in his most recent phase to have turned to a fundamental search for salvation, drawing back to his Jewish roots and a dialogue with his God.

It was one of my own students in the 60s at Cambridge who found his way through a study of Rimbaud out of a dream and fantasy world. He felt—in an essay I still prize—that he was struggling his way back to himself and to reality.

Rimbaud's decision to become a trader might be questioned. Perhaps Baudelaire is more significant for comparison with the singers and their fans of the 60s and after. Auden once commented on the phases Baudelaire passed through, in an introduction to the poet's *Intimate Journals*. He suggested that our European heritage presents urban romantics like Baudelaire with three models—two Greek and one Jewish. First, the rebel hero of the Greek poets, endowed with *arete*, flair and giftedness, struck down by the gods for his pride. Second, the seer of the Greek philosophers, endowed with an equally special knowledge and vision. Both transcend the fate of those round them, set apart from the herd. Like so many of his modern successors, Baudelaire tried out both faces until he recognised them for the masks they were. At length he came to the third, the biblical. Ordinary humble men like the patriarchs, the prophets or the disciples, like Job or Paul, hear the call and in their hearts trust and obey. It is a choice (unlike the hero and seer they are confronted with a choice) which leads them to suffering and to a love which is not, like so much 'pop' love, primarily a desire, but a costly giving of oneself to the needs of others.

Auden notes what he sees as a change of heart when Baudelaire sets himself in the last pages of his journal to write down his debts:

Jeanne 300, my mother 300, myself 300, 800 francs a month ... Immediate work, even when it is bad, is better than day-dreaming. To pray to God ... for life and strength for my mother and myself; to divide all my earnings—to obey the strictest principles of sobriety, the first being abstinence from any stimulants whatsoever.

It was just before his death. 'To the eye of nature,' says Auden, 'he was too late. As he spoke, the bird stooped and struck. But to the eye of the Spirit we are entitled to believe he was in time—for though the Spirit needs time, an instant of it is enough.'

Facing reality
So far this has been a western tale. But as technology with its unique power to separate and disintegrate spreads through the cities of the world and out to the ever more urbanized countryside, the story has a universal relevance. Everywhere, even in the West now, the young look out on a more bleak economic prospect of recession and unemployment. They seem likely to approach the future with more caution and scepticism about leaders, gurus, slogans, solutions, words, even, than their predecessors. It may be duller to be a student now than in the 60s. But you may have the opportunity of making a more mature assessment of the choices confronting you.

From within the pop mystical tradition and yet reaching beyond it came Robert Pirsig's *Zen and the Art of Motor-cycle Maintenance*. He tries to resolve the romantic/rationalist dilemma, and to bring together the spiritual and the technical aspects of life. He shows with fresh force what Michael Polanyi pointed out so powerfully, the close similarity if not identity between the scientific and artistic creation. In passages like the brilliantly entertaining discussions of the instructions for the assembly of an outdoor barbecue rotisserie and other mechanisms, 'Assembly of Japanese bicycles requires great peace of mind' he illuminates the nearness of the skills of a mechanical technician and, say, a sculptor. All this is conveyed as he journeys on a motor-cycle searching for himself. And yet, in the end, it remains the isolated exploration of the seer in search of his mystic secret, concrete yet abstract as a Zen Master's koan. He surely comes nearer to the truth when suddenly, towards the end, be breaks through to his son, lonely companion of his journey, till that moment excluded from the trip.

The truth he really finds then is what Dylan, Lennon, my student friend, are struggling for when they want to 'get down to reality'. The real unifying theme of our life, of reason and feeling, technician and ordinary man, public and private worlds, is our personal nature. As John Macmurray pointed out long ago the secret of true rationality and of right feeling are one and the same. It is in discovering how to be genuinely and unselfishly and humbly objective that we arrive at the true quality of great art and great science, of right and mature human relationships and of a right social order. Here we need to concentrate our analysis and our action. Here we can harvest the ultimate fruits of the upheaval of the 60s, a society, socialist or capitalist, 'with a human face'.

And the Christian claim is that, in humble and honest repentance, coming to this personal truth is bound up with the encounter 'in Christ' with the Personal God. From this encounter can flow out a practical concern and a political commitment with a spiritual source, a faith for the humane and for the human.

This very material reality is being discovered and demonstrated by young people in every part of the world. Students in industrial training centres in Kenya or at Gujranwala in Pakistan for whom technical training combined with biblical teaching in an atmosphere of practical faith has meant they have often discovered a purposeful integrity in their approach to work or to social justice. A young pastor and his wife and a missionary social worker have helped boys and girls in a diocesan centre in East Africa to come in out of street gangs and find their way into a new relationship with God and each other. Students whom I have met on journeys through Asia and East Africa talk and pray together of their future, facing their problems and those of their people realistically and yet hopefully with a directness of faith that shamed me. Evangelists like Bernard, a young Kenyan, with his group of 'evangelistic guerrillas' as they are called, people whose simplicity of life and quiet practicality are genuinely impressive. All over the world, the Churches of the poor can show us such.

From our own country, just to mention one group among many, our young CMS volunteers, who have learnt so much from fellow Christians overseas, have discovered in a variety of roles, in Kenya, in Iran, in India, that (as one of them working in a boys' hostel put it) 'God has more to do in us than through us', and thus demonstrated unwittingly the inherent realism of their faith.

A few have served in one of the most unexpected settings in small communities, set up in Asia by the founders of 'The Ark' in Amsterdam, and each known as 'Dilaram House' (house 'of the peaceful heart' in Farsi). These cater for wanderers on the hippie trail who come to India in search of enlightenment. Drop-outs who drop in meet an easy, flowing way of life, colourful rooms, a host 'family' in jeans or robes indistinguishable from their own. Only gradually through the strong feeling of acceptance, the songs, the talk and the laughter, an underlying rhythm and discipline make themselves felt. Those who remain long enough can begin to sense the point at which painfully, but also joyfully, we have come to the end of ourselves, even of the luxury of our own questing, to drop all the ultimately phoney faces we have been trying on, to be brought face to face with the inexorable compassion, inescapable justice and tenderness of the One whose truth and whose forgiveness will renew and reintegrate the life of us all, young and old together, and of our broken world.

Recommended Books

Peter L. Berger and others, *The Homeless Mind.*
Lennon Remembers (Pelican, 1973).
Jann Werner, *The Rolling Stone Interviews*, (Penguin, 1970).
Anthony Scaduto, *Bob Dylan*, (Abacus, 1972).
Baudelaire, *Intimate Journals*, (Methuen, 1949).
Robert M. Pirsig, *Zen and the Art of Motor-cycle Maintenance*, (Corgi, 1976).
Floyd McCung Jr., with Charles Paul Conn, *Just Off Chicken Street*, (Fleming H. Revell, New Jersey, USA, 1975).
John Macmurray, *Reason and Emotion*, (Faber, 1962).

A People Between

One late afternoon on one of my journeys to Japan, I was taken to a little wooden tea-house on the slopes of the hills above Kyoto, the ancient capital of Japan. Around us a fringe of the woods, the last golden leaves of the autumn shining with the fire of the sun's great red orb touching the horizon.

The mountain

Everything was significant: the water in the pool outside, the iridescent carp which flitted within it, the stepping stones we had crossed, the low door, the overhang of the roof, even the special implements which our hostess brought reverently in and arranged as she bowed and knelt. We were meant to appreciate each movement, each detail—the tiny marzipan emblems of autumn, leaves, mushrooms and pine-needles, and the deliberately roughened irregularity of the pottery cups, to be handled sensitively.

This was a time and a setting in which the participant was intended to look inward. It spoke with a wistful yearning for the essence of things, the reality beyond the illusion, which Buddhism had promised. Transcendence here, as in so much of Japanese spirituality, has been broken down into manageable fragments. The emphasis is on that atomising tendency in Buddhism which sees the stream of life as a succession of moments. The moment is the only concrete reality. The whole complexity of experience is reduced to a single point in which its true nature can suddenly be seen. We live for that *satori*, the surprise flash of inner insight.

Here truth is found nearest to the natural surfaces of life. There was something of the Confucian frugality and austerity of the mediaeval warrior, something of the Zen Buddhist simplicity and inwardness, something of the original Shinto nature divinities' harmony with their surroundings. It could appeal to those who might inwardly flee the material abundance, the machined regularity, of contemporary Japan.

As you look over the plain from the mountain towards the city, with its grey throng of concrete walls, narrow roads, packed apartments, you realise that even there a thousand occupants treasure the tiny landscape gardens of their miniature trees and plants, their fish, their insects. Here, too, the minuteness of the scale is partly a response to urban living, partly the capacity to see a 'world in a grain of sand', with the same passion with which so many cherish their inner pursuits—dance, painting, pottery, poetry—or hug to themselves memories of excursions into the hills; intimate longings for meaning beyond the daily pattern of work and social obligation which presses in upon them.

And the city
Swiftly the car swept us back into the traffic and on to one of the superb highways. Even Kyoto with its beautiful fringe of temples, shrines and palace soon merges into the morass of featureless modern buildings, the continuous urban blight cluttering the long narrow plain between sea and mountains. This seems a country with 'a sense of beauty but no sense of ugliness', as a friend put it. But then so much of the land is mountainous that only a tiny percentage is habitable. Even the smallest valleys and coastal strips were densely packed, crammed with fields or houses close together, with a stunningly high population. Modern industrialisation has intensified the process beyond belief, until 120 millions are pressed into a staggeringly small space.

No wonder the Japanese have had to master the skills of living together. At three crucial moments in their history they have absorbed and brilliantly redeveloped input from the outside world: first in the seventh-century importation of Chinese culture, second in the famous Meiji restoration when young modernisers used the name of the boy emperor to bring in western styles of government, education, industrialisation and militarisation, third in 1945 when, in the wake of defeat, the American occupation brought in a new phase of the ancient merchant tradition reinforced by a new materialism. Out of the economic boom that followed has arisen a fresh mutation of this always highly organised and homogenous culture.

In the underground station subways and shopping areas of cities, commuters stream past. All seems clean and shining, smooth, functioning, well-planned. The crowds are cheerful, purposeful, punctilious (except when it comes to pushing into rush-hour trains!). There is a feeling of well-ordered uniformity. Time is measured out in sections given to the groupings to which people owe so much dutiful energy and in which they find their reward. If there is a muted rat-race it is the struggle for and between groups. It begins early, with a struggle to find a place in the right schools; the strain distorts the content of education, often, and can affect the students' health. The successful have then to find the right business to enter and to remain in for life; for men, the right process up the ladder with their contemporaries; for girls, there is usually an end to a career at 25. Everything about business is marvellously organised, from the annual quite tough negotiations with the unions to the finely tuned intermeshing with government.

Your life is controlled by where you belong. In exchanging cards, men reveal first their business firm, then their rank within it, and only last their names. Even your leisure time is given up to pursuits undertaken in little hierarchical groups—your holiday tour, your excursion, your golf or your poetry making. This seems to be why people so often seem to suppress their resentments or their differences, polish the rough edges, soften the corners. Perhaps it is required that they conform.

Yet there is a haunting strain of individual passion somewhere. You sense it above all in the young—not only in the mass protests of a few years ago or in the untypical extremist groups, though it is there. But in some deeper inner restiveness dissatisfied with the rigid imprisoning of social constraint. It may come out in the writing of a diary or in the passion of many for novels in the first person, exploring a character's most intimate aspirations.

Where can there be an integration of the external world and this inner yearning? The famous New Religions offer, very successfully, only yet another grouping for those who feel themselves on the fringes of the main groups. They offer a spiritual means of attaining success in this life and group support. To many people, Buddhism is part of the conventional background of life and offers a funeral service with its little urban temples packed round with graves. Shintoism is mainly for weddings, an occasional half-superstitious prayer, like a coin thrown into a wishing-well in Britain, or a festival. The Christian Churches with a mere one per cent of the population have been influential purveyors of western education, popularising at least a notion of Christianity through, for instance, carols and Handel's *Messiah* at Christmas, so that the Bible and the story of Christ are surprisingly widely known. But perhaps the Church often seems too western and too alien to join. At best it is one more kind of leisure club, but one with a very high entry cost: 'the threshold is too high' as they say. Its schools may be prestigious, and may soften the strains of education, and its western missionaries be desired as teachers of English much in demand, but where can something more of Christ the Mediator, with his essential message to a split-level universe, be found?

Everywhere in little, largely hidden, ways lie the seeds of an answer, wherever the gospel is being deeply planted and genuinely reared and realised in Japanese soil. Ayako Miura's writings give us one vital clue. In her autobiography the characters write little poems to each other. The yearning is there, even the 'I' character revealing the depths of her longings. No wonder her books and films are so popular. But for those who can respond she also reveals a new love leaping out through the Christians she met in healing ways and spanning the divide between inner and outer, private and public, individual and social reality. There emerges an entirely Japanese but also universal pattern of discipleship.

Here and there in Japan are churches which are not just one more leisure club, but have a whole impact as a new community (a word which strangely has no counterpart in Japanese). The episcopal (Nippon Sei Ko Kai) housing estate church which its members built with their own hands between Tokyo and Yokohama and ran without a priest, sitting on *tatami* (mats) on the floor, now multiplying house meetings, touching many lives in a freshly integrating way. And everywhere, in the Christian schools too and more conventional churches, individuals come to a faith which affects their whole life and witness. The tiny mission house in a housing estate on the outskirts of Hokkaido, the student ministry in the university there or at Rikkyo University in Tokyo—all these begin to disclose Christ as the One whose moment does not break outside time and history but rather gives them meaning and gathers them in, the One who is found and followed as much in the structures of the city as on the mountain.

Rich world, poor world

Japan's material growth has had a negative impact outside the country. The very internal strengths of this society, its homogeneity, its single style of language and writing, the uniformity of its culture, have given it a signal separateness; for all their marvellous powers of adaptation from without, Japanese seem conscious of a sense of difference. If they have a sense of identity with anywhere beyond Japan, it is with America and Western Europe rather than with the great centres of Asian population so close to them. Moreover they are becoming conscious of a precarious dependence on external relationships. As the world's largest importers of oil, iron ore, lead, wood, cotton, heavily dependent both for energy and for food upon outside sources, they desperately need a peaceful and co-operative world.

Yet they seem ill-equipped to secure it, cut off by language, by script, by culture, by sheer incomprehension in a world which is insular but no longer isolated. Their East Asian neighbours resent them sharply. It was a shock to Japanese in the war when their armies were not welcomed as liberators but instead hated, when they were regarded as militarists. It was even more of a shock when Prime Minister Tanaka on a goodwill trip in 1974 met with an explosion of hatred of these 'economic animals' as they were harshly termed, ruthless, exploitative. We in the West are inclined to suspect them of flooding us heedlessly with their subsidised exports.

Both East and West feel that, since the war, Japan has been enjoying the benefits of growth without the responsibilities. And yet surely they should be mediators between the rich world of which they are now members and the poor world to which their tradition and historical setting might bind them. Are not sharp questions about growth posed by the inequalities of the world of the whole nature of Japanese society, to its conduct and relations with its neighbours, as much as to the West? Many younger Japanese seem alive to such questions and are feeling for a new approach.

Here again, Christians in Japan have found a special calling, not only in the Christian Council's concern for social issues or in the outstanding ministry of at least one church to Korean immigrants, minority sufferers within Japan. I am thinking of a less consciously political, even more spontaneous corporate and spiritual, response by young Christians—for instance, through work camps. One example was the pilgrimage of some students from Rikkyo University to a village in the Philippines to dig and to build, and eventually to befriend the reluctant villagers in a way which touched the lives of them all. 'We Japanese,' said their leader, Father Ogho, chaplain at Rikkyo, 'are like the poor lepers I once saw at Okinawa, victims of a poverty we helped to cause, for, like them, we are unable to feel pain where we should. In the Philippines we found the real meaning of the Cross and Resurrection of Christ for Japan—and for the world.'

One of the most striking little Christian communities I have visited anywhere was the Asian Christian Rural Institute in the foothills of the mountains some 100 miles from Tokyo, under its inspired and inspiring leader, Dr Takami. His is a group of rural workers from all over Asia, many of them quite poor and little qualified in the world's eyes, learning simply to live together and farm together, working out something of Japan's original skill brought into the setting of 'in Christ'. As I listened to them talking that evening, they opened windows, threw shafts of light, on differing Asian Christian scenes. With a characteristically Japanese and Christian sensitivity, humility and shrewdness, Dr Takami said to me: 'Japan will gain salvation only by giving itself to others.'

Early next morning we went round the farm. I was not surprised to learn that Dr Takami had had his schooling in a Zen monastery before he became a Christian. His perceptive questioning, his cherishing of every detail, reflected it. He cared gently for each part of the farm, and gave each person—especially the quietest and most diffident—their full weight. There was something of that tea ceremony I began with about it, but with a difference. Here the breakthrough was a new way of living which had immediate relevance for the practical surface city world. In the crucified Lord, the sharing community could become a mediating community between inner and outer, individual and collective, rich world and poor world—a picture of what, in Christ, Japan (and not only Japan) could become.

Recommended Reading
Edwin Reischauer, *The Japanese*, (Harvard University Press, 1978). My indebtedness to this book will be obvious.
Ayako Miura, *The Wind is Howling*, (Hodder & Stoughton, 1976).

Ayako Miura, *Shiokari*, (Overseas Missionary Fellowship, 1974).
Daniel C. Buchanan, *One Hundred Famous Haiku*, (Japan Publications Inc., 1973; obtainable through International Book Distributors, Hemel Hempstead, Herts.).
Haiku are the special 17-syllable poems composed by many Japanese.
Joan Giroux, *The Haiku Form*, (Charles Tuttle, 1974).
Smith Bradley (ed.), *Japan: a history in art*, (Simon & Schuster, 1974.)

Credibility Test

No one who heard the actor Alec McCowan read St Mark's gospel in one sitting can forget the freshness, the directness, the strangeness of its impact. At once I recognised the quality of countless versions of the gospel being preached, talked about and lived in the many little churches of the poor of our own time, often in obscure villages or shanty towns in Africa, Asia or South America, where that original good news is being rediscovered.

The real good news
It is not surprising that the gospel emerged in a similarly fresh form before the astonished eyes of Father Vincent Donovan, Roman Catholic priest, when he went to some of the Maasai, the great nomadic cattle herders of East Africa, to attempt what could seem to a Westerner, an almost new kind of mission. He aimed, without benefit of any material aid, without offering even the simplest schooling, medicine, even rural development, simply to sit down and talk about faith in Christ.

The Maasai response, after twenty years of good work by Roman Catholic schools and hospitals in the area had had little apparent effect, was startling. 'Who can refuse to talk about God? . . .' 'If that is why you came here, why did you wait so long to tell us about this? Why have you not come before?'

In the long months that followed of regular weekly discussions with people of five settlements summoned by their chief, the gospel and the church which sprang from it took their own essential form out of the interplay between the message of the God disclosed in Jesus and its new situation. Much of this form was distinctly Maasai, an incorporation of Maasai symbols—spittle expressing forgiveness or a tuft of grass peace—into a new pattern framed by baptism and eucharist. It could even appear in the view of its shapers as a preservation of the best of their own past. The simple force of their mode of worship, and some of their key themes, the pastoral nomadic setting, and Father Vincent's utter economy of presentation and demand, the mere planting of a seed to take root and sprout as it will within this new soil, bring sharply into question much of the mode of operation of traditional Christian mission and of Westernised Church life. There it is a kind of imprinting of the cross on the very fibre of Maasai community life. Father Donovan learns when to stop and leave his hearers to make the gospel their own. Baptism of the whole grouping becomes their moment of final assumption of responsibility, without any encumbrance of building, institutions or outside supervision or aid. A nomadic people is gradually transformed into an autonomous, Spirit-led pilgrim church, with its own strikingly original leaders and ministers, women as well as men, beginning to reach out to other Maasai with their message.

But there is one impressive way in which the gospel from the outset brings about a drastic break with the past. It impinges visibly at the moment when Father Vincent begins his preaching with the story of Abraham being called to renounce all localised territorial tribal gods and go out in search of the God of *all* tribes and nations. This makes an immediately costly demand. 'Perhaps Engai (the Maasai God) has become trapped in this Maasai country, among this tribe. Perhaps God is no longer free here. Perhaps you Maasai must also leave your nation and your tribe, at least in your thoughts, and go in search of . . . the God of all tribes.'

Later, in one village, a Maasai woman remarks: 'I think I understand what your message is saying to us. You are telling us we must love the people of Kisangiro (a village three miles away but a different clan). Why must we do that?' This was for her the giant step, the testing point of the gospel. When it came to the story of Jesus, again it was his opening up by word and deed, in parables and sayings for which Father Vincent found telling Maasai equivalents, which had the effect. He showed us the God who loved not only the Maasai, nor only the rich, the powerful, the healthy, the insider but the God who loves all, who is especially open to the poor, the weak, the sick, the outcast and excluded, calling us to love all people, to love our enemies. It was that very inclusiveness which brought him to the cross. And from his bearing of the cost of our separatedness spring 'the new Man' (Ephesians 1:15), the new people, the beginning of a new world.

This was the theme which burst all the bonds of Maasai, or of any other, cultural concepts, which put a new future tense into the language, which created new images like the 'age group' (the set or brotherhood into which each Maasai generation separately was incorporated) 'orporor' of God, lasting until the end of this age, and growing to include people of all clans and tribes. This was the 'new commandment' of St John's Gospel through which, as the disciples obeyed, all men would know, would believe (John 13:34 and 17:21). For Paul, the essential implication of grace, as contrasted with the Law, was that it opened up God to all, Jew and Greek, slave and free, male and female, *all* 'Abraham's offspring' by faith (Galatians 3:28), all even now sharing the same 'new nature' (Colossians 3:10, 11). In this extraordinary new Maasai Church there were immediate consequences. Previously separated groups came together, women sat at the breaking of bread and shared with men. Some of them confessed to Father Vincent that this brought home to them as nothing else that Jesus really was good news for them, that they had an equal place in his love.

In all such new churches the miraculous freshness and power of the message of Christ seem to carry similar drastic consequences. It is, as well, the essential motif and implication of the gospel in Don Richardson's amazing account of his attempt to convey the Christian faith to the stone-age Sawi people, head-hunting cannibals in New Guinea. Here inter-group tensions and conflicts ran so deep that treachery of a skilful and ingenious kind won admiration as a heroic act. When Richardson unfolded the story of Jesus he found it was Judas, not Jesus, who for the Sawi was the centrally attractive and impressive figure. He found himself searching in vain the intricacies of Sawi thought and ritual for some point of connection, for what he called a 'redemptive analogy'.

But there at length he stumbled on the strange and fascinating institution of the 'peace child', by which an infant child from each of two hostile villages was given to the other to be brought up there as a kind of sacred hostage. Peace would be preserved so long as both lived, and then the ritual of exchange was celebrated in a dance of mutual peace embrace, 'you-in-me, I-in-you': each circle moving in turn round the other. It was enough when violence broke out in the future to lay a hand upon the peace child and so recall the pledge. From this, Richardson was able at last, in the face of a touching readiness, to interpret Jesus as God's 'peace child' for all mankind, to be united in him with God and with each other.

Fellowship of the unlike

Such is the vividly experienced mark of the gospel wherever it finds fresh and full expression among peoples coming to it new. But then, the innocent questions probe the messengers like searchlight beams painfully scanning the churches from whence they come. 'Ah,' exclaims one of the Young Sawi warriors to Richardson, 'You Tuans (whites) never war with each other, so of course you don't need a peace child!' A Maasai elder asks Father Donovan: 'This story of Abraham—does it speak only to the Maasai? Or does it speak also to you?' Donovan, who seems much more aware than Richardson of the awkward questions which the new-found faith of those he goes to raises for the church in his own country, after reflecting deeply on the tribal nature of Western religion, has to answer stumblingly to the Maasai: 'No, we have not found Him. My tribe has not known him. Let us search together. Maybe together we will find him'—something he had not meant to say. The same elder remarks: 'The High God of whom you speak could not possibly love Christians more than pagans, or he would be more a tribal god than ours.'

Tragically, a few removes from that first marvellous freshness of discipleship, division enters in. The fellowship of the *un*like, which is the mark of those who live out of the original gospel of grace, rapidly fades. Overall the norm is a church riddled everywhere with the same ethnic and regional tensions as the world round about it. In many ways, social and economic change has helped to develop and strengthen 'tribalism' which is so often, in its present virulence, a modern development. The church has not on the whole witnessed to a convincing new love or new forgiveness because it is itself conformed to the same processes, the same competitive enmity, which has influenced others. Sometimes it even intensifies them by making them denominational. Catholic and Protestant conflicts in particular have reinforced and added to political and social division, for example in Uganda or Eastern Nigeria where they have become part of history.

It is the same story in Asia. In India there have always been great hopes in the church, as in the mystic 'renouncer' sects, that caste would be transcended. Indeed it was largely (contrary to McGavran's thesis), the mixed nature of the Church, at least potentially, which in the past attracted the mass movements of the casteless people to the gospel in search not so much of rice, as an old cheap jibe suggests, as of dignity, respect and a new quality of life 'in Christ'. But caste and regional rivalries have from the beginning pervaded the Church.

We Western Christians, as Father Donovan rightly recognises, often present the most tragic obstacle of all to Christian belief. I am not thinking only of the behaviour of some white Christians dominated like most of us by fear and short-sighted self-interest in Southern Africa. I am not thinking so much, either of the way in which the Church in the United States has been shot through with racism of which the Black Muslim movement let alone Black Theology are eloquent symptoms. At least the legacy of Martin Luther King, among others, remains a vivid counter symbol for many of us. Again, while Ireland is the most tragic epitome of Christian failure, about which fellow Christians all over the world question me anxiously often, yet the hidden story of the Spirit's moving in the faithful self-sacrifice of some ordinary Christians working for reconciliation there, which seldom, mercifully for its continuance, appears in the news, offers its own alternative testimony.

The innocent questions of new Christians on the frontiers, whether here among the new disciples of all races in some inner-city groups or in the Third World, must come most painfully home to us in Britain. Our churches for the most part are still failing even in their own life and worship to demonstrate that new love, that profound sharing and forgiveness and forgivingness, which are the supreme mark of Christ's true church. Even the vital, growing charismatic and renewed churches, often in the suburbs, are not really yet places where anyone could at once sense a clear difference from the world in this area of class and race.

I believe there is a growing and genuine willingness on the part of British Christians to become emotionally identified with tough missionary situations overseas. But are we yet willing to become deeply involved with the church's mission in inner city, housing estates and working-class areas of Britain, not paternalistically but with a genuine readiness to be changed ourselves? Are we willing to witness to that potentially more class-free and multiracial Britain so deeply and sadly repudiated in much of our national life and even some of our recent legislation?

Only one way left
Mercifully, within the Church here as elsewhere, there is 'far back through creeks and inlets making' a quietly pervasive movement of a new tender and realistic love, flowing from a Living Source. Clergy and laity alike are

doing much steady work unpublicised and only jeopardised by some new demonic outburst or upheaval of all-too-prevalent fear or hate. There are groups and networks spreading of those committed to the rediscovery of this real gospel life, with the genuine and unmistakable quality of the fruit of the Spirit about it. They are working for a genuinely revived church with a fuller gospel engendering, in those who receive Christ through it, the power to challenge our whole sick social system with all its false values in such a way that it both touches many individual lives and expresses in its very being a gospel to 'the structures' of society. Surely we could see a model for the Church everywhere in the world in the words of J. B. Webster writing about the Church in India:

It may be a necessary priority for the Church to present in whatever context it is placed alternatives to certain dominant norms and values . . . in an impersonal city, it should be a caring community; where parochialism and rivalry of caste or language or region are rampant, it should be a place of openness and unity; among the rich and powerful it should champion the underdog; where hierarchies of caste or class or sex prevail, it should be a place where all are equal; when set among the poor and oppressed it should build up a sense of dignity and self confidence. (*NCC Review* vol C no. 19, p497)

One of the clearest embodiments of this gospel to me is the Zebra Project, a Christian team working to bring people, and frequently Christian people, of different races together. Their work with congregations up and down the country provides us with something of a model. They help local people to arrange meetings and visits between black and white Christians, to share experiences and a willingness to expose underlying hurt or anger in an atmosphere in which people have sometimes found previously held opinions toppled and new insights gained. They have begun to glimpse the reality into which Christ yearns to bring us, and without which it is hardly possible for the whole to know or to believe the reality of the Peace Child, of God's age group, into which the Sawi and the Maasai can still lead even us.

Recommended reading
Vincent J. Donovan CSSp, *Christianity Rediscovered: An Epistle from the Maasai* (Fides/Claretian, Notre Dame, Indiana 1978).
Don Richardson, *Peace Child* (G/L Regal Glensdale, California, 1979).
Face to Face: a Programme for Multi-racial Education and other materials, The Zebra Project, Bow Mission, Merchant Street, London E3.

African Mediator

The Granada Television film *Witchcraft Among the Azande*, the first in a *Disappearing World* series, early in 1982 gave some fascinating glimpses of a part of Sudan already familiar to some, at least, of the audience. It was the area made familiar to the readers of Evans Pritchard, the great anthropologist, in his classic study of the 'last stand' of a closed, self-explaining world, *Witchcraft, Oracles and Magic among the Azande*, published in 1937.

The frustration of Father Jerome

In the film you could see and experience people attempting to discover the deep cause of illness or misfortune, to predict success or failure, and to detect guilt or prove innocence, by consulting oracles. A man rubbed pieces of wood together to see whether the pieces stuck or moved freely; drove two branches into an anthill to see whether one or both were eaten by the morning; and ultimately Benge, the poison oracle, was consulted. You saw the poison being applied to small chickens, the death of which proved one woman guilty of witchcraft, so that she had to cleanse herself by spitting water. Another woman was convicted of adultery by the same oracle in a local chief's court and made to pay a fine.

But there were significant differences between the Azande world shown here and that of Evans-Pritchard's book. The focus of the scene had shifted. The traditions, now a little frayed and shabby, were somehow more peripheral. New forces were at work. Somewhere outside the picture there was a new centre, while in the village

itself a Church had appeared to which many of the people
went. A younger generation still deferred to the elders to
an extent, but they seemed less certain. There was more
open drunkenness and immorality. We saw a young couple
purifying their new-born baby by the time-honoured
method of smoking it—holding it over a fire. We saw the
witchdoctor dancing out the cause of a failure in the hunt,
and learned that he was a practising member of the
church.

Finally, we met the African priest in charge of the
church. This was Father Jerome. He was the most
puzzling figure in the film both to the curious viewer and,
evidently, to all the villagers—possibly even to himself. He
professed to give no credence either to the oracles resorted
to by everyone else or to the alleged evils of which they
were supposed to be the cure—witchcraft and 'bad' medicine. He thus appeared at least to ignore the very real and
deep inner and social tensions symbolised and tackled,
after a fashion, by the traditional system. In the church
service we saw him endeavouring to persuade his congregation to accept his view of things with a blend of
westernised Christian orthodoxy and rationalism. In his
lonely struggle to uphold the educated values of his
seminary and of a more distant urban world, he seemed
brave but frustrated.

The great divide

All this brings us to the picture of one of the problems
facing the rapidly growing churches in Africa today, which
is presented in Adrian Hastings' *History of African
Christianity* as well as the work he helped to edit,
Christianity in Independent Africa. The same issue
emerged at a conference held in 1982, under the auspices
of the Royal Anthropological Institute, on Emergent
Christianity in Africa. Here, as in his books, Adrian
Hastings pointed to a divide, a great gulf, fixed between
the institutional centres of power and control in the
church, in the hands of a clerical or clericalised-lay
hierarchy, and the seething, ever-growing mass of small

local congregations in the countryside, or even high-density urban areas, 'less and less amenable to control from government or ecclesiastical superstructure'.

When it comes to this mass phenomenon, Dr Hastings suggests, the distinctions between catholic, protestant and independent may be less significant than studies of isolated churches would suggest. Students today might do well to pay less attention to *my* independent church, a notion which seems, in some religious studies circles, almost to have replaced the old anthropological *my* tribe as a source of research degrees, and to concentrate more on the African spiritual scene as a whole. The enormous growth of the Christian church, its numbers in sub-Saharan Africa now amounting to an estimated 150 million, needs more careful analysis. It includes a bewildering diversity of institutions, movements, symbolic systems.

Various attempts at an overall interpretation of what is happening in Africa as a whole have been made. The first and most outstanding anthropological interpreter was Robin Horton, well known for his articles in *Africa*, especially one entitled 'African Conversion' (*Africa*, Vol. XLI, 1971, pp 85–108). He sees Christianity as essentially a catalyst brought into a process which was already taking place within the whole world view of many African societies. These societies had developed with what were essentially *localised* religious systems. At the centre of such a system were fixed and localised spiritual powers, the ancestors or 'living dead' and the divinities which presided over the community as a whole. Further out on the fringes were the more free-ranging and dynamic spirits, often using for their mediums women or younger people, and by their very nature more ready to sponsor the unexpected or the new. Behind both was the overarching shadowy figure of a more comprehensive abstract divnity, embracing the universe as a whole and the wider world beyond the local society. As Western, or indeed Arab, intrusion opened up the smaller-scale societies of even the larger African cultures to a wider world, what may have happened was that local authorities were weakened, as

were the spirits which underpinned them. The more
universal divinity became far more significant. The free-
ranging spirits also attempted to move in more to the
centre of the scene as their mediums became the 'prophets'
of new cults and indeed new churches.

If the whole concept of the divine became widened, so
also did the concept of evil and of evil powers. The causes
of sickness or misfortune could now be diagnosed much
less as an offence against local rules and the spiritual
beings which had sanctioned them. They were much more
seen to be the work of a whole variety of often newly
discovered evil spirits afflicting individuals, frequently
including some of the previous local spirits but also adding
to them others from further afield. But a more generalised
disorder could be felt to be afflicting society as a whole,
and indeed the entire cosmos. This was associated with a
general 'prevalence of witches'. These two interpretations
of evil lent themselves to treatment by exorcism or by
some kind of witch-cleansing movement or church, with an
apocalyptic feel to it. In this way, then, the traditional
world view was being modified or developed in new
directions to cope with great social and political changes.
This was a process which was in train anyway. Christianity
flowed into it, became a part of it and, by introducing both
the Bible—the *book*, symbol of modernity—and links with
the wider church especially in the West, offered a new kind
of universality.

All this helps to explain the whole spectrum of seething
experiment, innovation and acceptance or rejection of
various aspects of Christianity in varying African settings.
It explains why it is often difficult now to define with any
clarity in Africa what is Christian and what is not.
Further, it explains the nature of the gulf between the
more westernised institutionalised centres of power in the
church, and the local and popular struggle to find healing
and new community where people are. The centre can often
be more westernised, more intellectual and, like Father
Jerome himself, more rationalistic and secularised in its
approach, content with a more divided world.

The masses are still happier with either a variety of prayer houses, clinics, centres of a praying and cleansing therapy, a Christianised equivalent perhaps of the oracles, the traditional healer or the 'free-ranging spirits' I mentioned as part of the old order. Occasionally, they may be swept into a whole prophetic healing or witch-cleansing movement, a complete counter-culture offering an alternative modernity. This is how large new independent churches have been born.

What seems to be lacking is some kind of mediation between this widely desired wholeness, bringing with it new community, new meaning and deliverance from the assault of evil powers, and the ordinary institutional church. That institutional church is itself controlled by a more educated, economically and politically powerful, urbanised middle class. With its more cerebral, sophisticated culture, it has strong links naturally with the West.

The quest for a mediator
What is needed, then, is some genuine mediation between the demon-haunted folk world of the pulsing vital periphery, and the too faint a reflection of the gospel so often presented in the respectable hierarchical centre. Perhaps what is really being looked for here, as in so many other parts of the world-wide church, is ultimately a fuller, more direct apprehension of Christ. The mediation we are looking for can only be provided by Christ himself. The heart of the symbolic problem lies in the absence of a real grasp upon Christ in the strength of his selfgiving, the conqueror of the powers of evil. In the true rediscovery in Africa of a more complete vision of Christ could lie the key to Africa's many spiritual movements.

This is what the pentecostalism of many independent churches in Africa and the whole East African revival movement have been feeling for. Joe Church's important autobiography has vividly reminded us of the crucial quest of that movement. These African Christians have been in search, as we are in the West, of the broken and glorious Christ in whom there can be a coming together of the historical, institutional centre of the church with the dynamic spiritual periphery. Here is the meeting of the cross and the Spirit, the fruit and the gifts, the ethical and the vitally experiential.

In certain significant figures in the African Church we have seen this mediation 'in Christ' between the institutional and the 'spiritual'. In the history of the East African revival, especially in Uganda, there have been many examples, from Blasio Kigozi to Janani Luwum and some of the refugees in Sudan. There have been men like Adam the Prophet of the church in Isoko in the Western Delta of Nigeria. He was, until his recent death, for a number of years a lay reader widely recognised for his healing and preaching gifts in the diocese of which he was a part, leading a singing, praying and evangelistic band with great power. There was the extraordinary and deeply impressive healing ministry a few years ago of Edmund John, brother of the then Archbishop of the Anglican church in Tanzania. His brother and other church leaders helped to organise the series of packed meetings in Maasai Cathedral and in other places at which, like Adam in Nigeria, John was at pains to deflect all attention from himself to Christ. For such preachers, the Christ of the mission-founded Churches stands forth as the wounded healer, the divine Nganga, who stands between his people and all the evils which oppress and threaten them. He fights and wins the victory for them against all the powers of darkness. This is the Christ who must shine out at the centre of the local village community and equally at the institutional centre. We can surely draw the analogies and see some of the lessons for the church in the West.

Clearly the future of our own church hangs on our fresh grasp on and obedience to that vision of Christ which we also have to find and communicate afresh. Certainly, also, the future of that enormously variegated and vigorous phenomenon, loosely called 'Christianity in Africa', will depend on how far it can find its true centre in Christ in his fulness.

That fulfilment will only be realised where the church

becomes the genuine Body of such a Christ. In Joseph Healey's book *A Fifth Gospel* (don't be put off by that rather misleading title) he describes the emphasis that Bishop Christopher Mwoleka, a man of great humility and simplicity of life, puts on staying simply among the poorest members of his own village whenever he can. There is a very definite attempt here to affirm the authority and gift of each simple member of the group of farmers and labourers. Father Healey described some of them poignantly. In such a setting, with such genuinely self-abnegating leadership, the forgiving and healing power of Christ can become part of the lived and felt experience of the village. Christ the Mediator can find African form.

In a way, Africa's quest is our quest too. And we need each other's help to find its right fulfilment in Christ.

Recommended reading
Edward Fashole Luke and others (eds.), *Christianity in Independent Africa* (Rex Collings, London, 1978).
A History of African Christianity 1950–1975, (Cambridge University Press, 1981).
Joseph G. Healey, *A Fifth Gospel* (SCM Press, London, 1981).
Joe Church, *Quest for the Highest* (Paternoster, London, 1982).

Tale of Two Cities: Christians in Hong Kong and Singapore

As the great wing dipped, suddenly a turn of the bare grey coastline revealed the always surprising sight, the sudden rash of clustered tower blocks within the curve of the shore and sprawling along the narrow valley behind the hills, the harbour and, packed together, springing to meet us, fully formed, the glossy skyscrapers on the island itself. There it lay, improbable as a mirage of the future, emerging from the grey haze, Hong Kong, poised on the edge of China.

Hong Kong—overcoming contradictions
Was it just the mist-wraiths swirling, was it that new sense of the precariousness of it that brought to mind

> The cloud capp'd towers, the gorgeous palaces,
> The solemn temples, the great globe itself,
> Yea, all which it inherit, shall dissolve
> And, like this insubstantial pageant faded,
> Leave not a rack behind . . . ?

But that hint of transience soon itself gave way to a solid enough encounter with the striking airport runway between the buildings; the tunnel road under the water; the teeming streets with their many jostling signs in English or Chinese; the vibrant purposeful crowds coming and going on the Mass Transit Railway with its strictly functional, metallic carriages, opening into each other so that you can look right down the inside of the train from one end to the other. Conversations with some of the many younger passengers could open into a world where people are used to hardships, to long hours, to cherished dreams, buried hopes and fears, in a scene in which power and wealth lie in the hands of others. There the lure of the endless struggle to make it in a place where there is just enough schooling, just enough of a job, of a thinly stretched medical service or a foothold in a tenement block, to press on.

Hong Kong can fairly be depicted as a brilliant commercial success, a show-case for *laissez-faire* capitalism, with its almost legendary prosperity, responsiveness to the market, entrepreneurial flair. A western and westernised community, it can be a goose that lays the golden eggs for mainland China itself and must be kept capable of doing so in the future.

At the same time you can point to the gap between the few rich and the many poor, the concentration of power and policy-making in the hands of a few, the moral disintegration of which prostitution, gambling, robbery, drugs and alcohol are the symptoms, the lack of real job security or social justice, let alone of basic political rights—all symptoms of a spiritual void.

China is as much caught up in this basic conflict as Britain, or the people of Hong Kong themselves. For long, China has wanted the recovery of sovereignty over Hong Kong and was determined to obtain this. But the last thing the Chinese government would desire would be to do anything to damage the fruitfulness of an economy in which it already has such a major stake. The device of creating 'one country—two systems' and making Hong Kong a 'Special Administrative Region', theoretically autonomous except in external foreign or defence matters, and with its own executive, legislative and judiciary powers, was worked out in order to keep much of the *status quo*. In an amazing treaty the present Chinese government under Zhao Zhiyang (and of course Deng Xiaoping) has promised little change, much the same rights, laws and economic freedom as now for 50 years at least. Hong Kong is to be internally run by its own citizens, even if the Chief Executive and senior officials are to be nominated.

At the same time China must needs consolidate its control over the city in 1997. Chinese troops are to be stationed in Hong Kong. There is to be a new 'Basic Law' or constitution with which everything at present happening has to be brought into line, and no one knows quite what this may contain. It is not even clear that the present régime in China interprets human rights or 'free speech' in the same way as the West. Already the Chinese have distanced themselves from hesitant British attempts at introducing a very partial and indirect democracy.

Were the British to do what they really should and introduce full-blooded democracy, it could equally threaten present business interests and future Chinese government interests. In the hand-over, Hong Kong citizens may well find their freedom squeezed between British and Chinese régimes as they exchange one domination for another.

Some see the experiment as potentially a brilliant success, a model for divided countries such as East and West Germany or South and North Korea. Such hopes accompanied the first release of the White Paper and its wide distribution, well over a million copies in the city. There is a feeling that the contradictions can be reconciled by high economic growth, that the global human conflict between freedom and control, the apparently inexorable dilemma of liberty or equality, would be almost magically resolved at last in this one Shangri-La.

But, strangely, young people in post-Maoist China itself, conscious of a certain cultural and political breakdown of ideals, tend to look West, much as some of their western counterparts have looked East! Perhaps they, too, are more aware of the basic incompatibility of the two semi-western forms, capitalism and Marxism, into which Chinese in varied settings have poured their considerable energy and skill. 'I know of no place on earth,' wrote one scholarly Chinese observer, 'where two distinct political entities as vastly different as capitalist Hong Kong and communist China are able to settle down together in harmony.' No one even knows—and this is one of the greatest fears—what the leadership in China will be like by 1997. The present rulers will probably be dead by then. That half of the Hong Kong population who are refugees from Maoist China tend to be among the pessimists. They may, like their counterparts in West Germany, South Korea or Taiwan, be sharply aware of the shorcomings of the West. But they know with a grim realism a situation that can be worse still.

Christians in Hong Kong share in all these contradictory expectations and fears. They must needs look for continuity. They would cling to the rule of law and to religious freedom. The Chinese may allow them to continue to run schools and the extensive social service agencies, as they do at present with government subsidy. But perhaps the syllabus will be controlled, and the government's grip on all they do will tighten. The Churches could be over-stretched, and unable to supply sufficient truly Christian staff to give their schools the quality they require.

They all hope, while remaining denominational, to strengthen relationships with Christians (now non-denominational) in China itself so that Churches in Hong Kong might make a significant contribution to modernisation and 'social reform'. Bishop K. H. Ting, President of the China Christian Council in mainland China, was recently in Hong Kong announcing to the world a new 'Amity Foundation', a 'secular' development body with a largely Christian committee, hoping to draw contributions of money and personnel from western Churches. Christians in Hong Kong could join in such a programme.

But again there is another factor. Sensitive Christians are aware of certain overtones of power and patronage about the Church in Hong Kong. Bodies like CMS have much to live down, as do the Churches, not least the Anglicans, from their colonial, commercial and missionary history. There are and have been many much-loved saints, apostles and servants, expatriate and Chinese. But the

Church can still appear to many local people as having a special affinity with a wealthy government and Westerners.

Some Christians look for a new role for a much leaner, more radical Church of the poor with a simpler life-style, leaving behind its 'institutional burdens' and working for a just and sharing society. There are also Evangelicals and Pentecostals who would look for the Church now to concentrate more on building up a flexible house-church structure, proof against all possible future onslaughts.

The trouble is that such 'stripping down' of the Church would consort awkwardly with other Hong Kong and future Chinese government expectations of maintaining the *status quo*, the capitalist style, the inherited pattern which makes Hong Kong what it is. Christians may want now to contribute to preparing people for democracy or to join in discussions on the future Basic Law. But Beijing may well want neither the democracy nor the discussions. They might even prefer the Church as it is, an efficient, voluntary social agency and proprietor of institutions.

One thing is clear. The Churches at the moment, while effectively organising in congregations the approximately 8% of the population who are Christians and running some excellent institutions and social projects serving many groups, are conscious of a certain lack. One traditional Church leader called it the 'genuinely spiritual dimension'. 'We are an "efficient machine",' he said.

Yet deep in the heart of the 'walled city', its dripping walls and dark cavernous workshops like an engraving of an early industrial inferno, a team of young Chinese converted drug addicts working with Jackie Pullinger, prayed over and tenderly cherished fellow victims, with a release of the Spirit, an uprush of *agape* love, which could heal and reshape broken lives.

One person commented to me: 'When the card houses of our world are shaken, these are the kind of people who will stand', and 'Strengthen the things that remain.'

We ourselves have much to learn from Christians in Hong Kong as they face 1997. They call upon us to stand by them in prayer, in encouragement in their efforts to develop new democratic patterns, and to enable them, through bodies like CMS, to join in new mission with other Churches all over the world in the years ahead.

Singapore—significant centre

Hegel was right. The one great underlying contradiction, that between the spiritual and the material, ideal and reality, has been resolved in Christ crucified and risen. Perhaps that is why the cities on which the coming world is converging present the deepest questions and the final opportunity for the Gospel of Christ to penetrate and fulfil all faiths. It was strange to descend again on another equally improbable centre—a green diamond-shaped island the size of the Isle of Wight but with a population of two and a half million. Its founder, Raffles, called it 'The navel of the Malay countries' and chose shrewdly, for it has become the main East-West shipping port and key air communications centre. Out of a British framework, decisively broken by the Japanese, and after a brief Malaysian interlude (1963–5), a largely expatriate Chinese enterprise finally became the base for an incredible industrial and commercial expansion. Lee Kuan Yew presided over this Asian 'miracle', whereby a confused fragment of humanity with small resources, a bleak international prospect and internal dissension, became a focal point of business and communications for the whole of East Asia. Its airport is one of the busiest in the world, its dollar as strong as the yen, its population at 2½ millions has more than doubled and 70% of its people are settled in post-war racially integrated housing projects.

Here at the heart of East Asia, in the midst of a growing modern city, you find a vigorously growing Church, which has risen from 2% to 12% of the population in the last 20 years. Even the Anglican Cathedral hums with life. In the tower blocks, house churches are multiplying. Everywhere you encounter lives being changed, and you are struck by a new quality of faith and prayer. The old folk-religions have been breaking up, the old-style *kampong* (village) life is fading. Even family ties are loosening a little. The social cost of high-rise high-density living is making itself felt. For the Churches there is a crucial ministry, a tremendous opportunity and vital resources in the Spirit. At every level, from that of wealthy entrepreneurs encountering the Full Gospel Businessmen to that of young office workers packing into a healing and evangelistic rally, there is a gospel dynamism touching lives.

Of course criticisms are made of this almost entrepreneurial spirituality. It is often individualistic and pietistic. It reaches the middle class and the educated more than the working people. Numbers of younger men especially pour into and then drop out of the Churches. People move from one Church to another in a pragmatic style in search of some specific ministry. There is much ministry but still too little to the disadvantaged, the elderly, the handicapped, the misfits. Businessmen can worship God on Sunday and return to the ruthless struggle on Monday without always relating the two.

Embodying the Spirit
All this may be true. Yet the fact remains that from first landing to leaving you meet Church members full of faith-love; learn of lives changed and healed through Christ's Spirit; meet business people who *have* changed their attitude to rivals or employees; find young people gathering together whose urgent eager witness and joy in the power of Christ ministering through them is touching—and catching. Something of vital moment and potential is happening here—something which, through a body like CMS, a western Church could share, and from which we have much to receive.

Through all this stirring, growing city, facing new questions, the Spirit in Christ must again seek to pervade and transfigure the material world of human struggle and pain, to refine and modify the economic thrust, to infuse all of reality with compassion and a longing to share every kind of good more widely. Christians here, as in Hong Kong, need to find an ever fuller, more deeply integrated calling. And as they wrestle in the midst of these great urban social and spiritual experiments, may we be enabled through an exchange of Christians between our Churches and theirs to share with them in that wrestling.

Recommended reading

Hong Kong

Pro Mundi Vita Dossiers, *Hong Kong 1997: a Historical Challenge for the Churches*, Asia-Australasia Dossier No 32, (Pro Mundi Vita, rue de La Lunite 6, B-1030, Brussels, Belgium).

A Draft Agreement on the Future of Hong Kong, Miscellaneous No 20, (HMSO, 1984).

Green Paper: *The Further Development of Representative Government in Hong Kong* (Hong Kong Government Office, 6 Grafton Street, W1).

A Boat within a Boat, excellent filmstrip available from Hong Kong Council of Churches.

Singapore

Bobby E. K. Sng, *In His Good Time*. The story of the Church in Singapore 1819–1978. Graduates' Christian Fellowship, Singapore 1980. (CMS Library) January 1986: CMS Project—Singapore Church presents story of its own growth and work.

PART III

Christ For The World

Missionary Movements: A New Phase

In many parts of the world Church, people are moving 'out from under' inherited or imposed institutions to discover new ways of worship and of life together. You find them in informal gatherings, house-meetings, cells, in settings somewhat removed from the ordinary activities of the Church. They may be in groups like the communal farm where rural workers from many countries developed their skills, above all in relationships, as they worked together under Dr Takami's inspiration. You will find them in renewal meetings, whether among Aboriginal Australian villagers meeting in the open air to sing and pray, in a youth camp in Calcutta, or in an afternoon gathering in a large church in Kigali, Rwanda.

Springs of revival

At once you realise that the movements that have stirred and spread the Church, exploding and expanding from within, have seldom, if ever, come from the top or worked their way through the formal structure downwards and outwards. From the beginning they have been spontaneous up-rushings of the life of the Spirit moving at will among particular people in particular places. In the New Testament the impetus came from the missionary apostles and inspired prophets, in the Early Church from the martyrs, then from the desert fathers, and in the Middle Ages from the monastic movements and their millenarian counterparts. Then came the lay mystical fellowships, the

Anabaptist radical reformation, the mystics and orders of the Counter-reformation. Finally there are the evangelical and catholic revivals of modern times, with liturgical and charismatic renewal, down to the new cells, teams and communities of Charles de Foucauld, of Taizé, of the Focolare. Alongside them also are the Jesus movements and the forceful transatlantic style of Operation Mobilisation or Youth with a Mission.

For all its occasional tragic divisions and distortions, the 'Balokole' (brotherhood) movement in East Africa has provided much of the energy for the astounding expansion of the Church in the whole area. Even in the ancient Churches of the East, episcopacy has had, from early days, its strange bond with monasticism—so much so that only a deep monastic revival can bring about a subsequent revitalisation of the Church, especially in the face of sharp persecution. This has been happening in Russia for some time, where the sources of renewed life have long lain deep in the *poustinia*, the hidden retreat of hermits and *staretsi*, holy men, in the forests. It is happening in Egypt where the present Coptic renewal has its springs in that most ancient of all hidden areas of encounter with God, the desert.

'Structure' and 'communitas'

In his book *The Ritual Process*, Vincent Turner reflected on the contrast between the formal, institutional aspects of human social life and its spontaneously free and formless moments and movements. He used the word 'structure' to describe the normal institutions, the constant patterns and rules by which human relationships are organised and ordered. By these means power is distributed, authority assigned and the varying functions of different members of society fixed. Above all there is some clear sense of differentiation and hierarchy. Such institutions may be manipulated by those who want to hold on to power. But at least those who live within such a framework are protected from chaos or disintegration. These institutions are required to protect us from our own frailty and fallibility (as Paul suggests in Romans 12). They provide continuity in time and in space. They permit society to function after a fashion. Cast them out as we may, they will, like ritual itself, return in one form or another.

But over against this 'structure', there come moments and places in the life of a society where there is a suspension of such patterns. All differences are deliberately expunged. There is a sudden feeling for an entirely *un*differentiated, egalitarian unity. This characteristic Turner called 'communitas'. Indeed, it arouses a sense of underlying communion and community, for which in any society there may be a profound yearning. Even for highly structured societies there may be certain moments when the exact converse of their normal experience comes into play, when all categories and labels are lifted, all rules reversed. There is something of this in such traditions as the ancient 'Feast of Fools' in which the jester is viewed as king. There may even be movements, within the wider framework of an hierarchical society, in which some of the more marginal people deliberately seek to find an alternative utopian equality of mutual sharing and caring. An attempt is made to bypass structures and to break through to an ideal state of pure undivided oneness where there are no separations. This ideal world can be imagined as coming out of the mythical past or lying in the future.

But the key point of the argument is that the two cannot really be alternatives. Structure and community in fact need each other. Ideally, moments of community can serve to cleanse and renew structure, and it should be the goal of structure itself to serve and help to realise community effectively. The forward thrust here comes from guerrilla movements which have a crucial relationship with the main army, loosening and decentralising its chains of command. Innovation or expansion are the work of free-ranging project groups, as in industry, where ideally they complement the modes of operation of central 'line' management.

Biblical faith reveals the place where structure and community truly meet. It was F. W. Dillistone, in *Structure of the Divine Society*, who explored the way in which two aspects of Israel (and, later, of the Christian Church)—the 'covenantal' or chosen committed community and the 'organic' or apparently natural given social order—complement each other. As the pilgrim desert people begin to settle in Canaan, Kingship, Temple and City can become valuable symbolic institutions. But then, as the decades pass, there is a danger of the pilgrim experience being lost. The 'schools of the Prophets' emerge as corporate reminders of the desert model. The 'organic' hierarchical structure has by now become distorted and corrupted in the hands of the powerful and wealthy.

It seems, therefore, as if covenanting bands, a faithful remnant, are needed before, during and after the Exile to recall Israel to its true vocation to be a vehicle of God's special choice and grace. Later such remnant communities become the only potential means of embodying the true Israel during the times of Hellenistic and Roman occupation. It is this true Israel that Jesus comes to call into being. In Jesus, ideal and reality meet, spirit and material form, 'heaven' and 'earth', are held together in his Cross and risen life. So his people, those who share that life, can be enabled in the Spirit to transcend the gulf betwen structure and community.

This kingdom-community of Jesus, for which the Church was to become at least a pointer and a sign, was not to destroy the institutions of Israel—Law, Sabbath, Temple, Kingship—but it was to reorientate and fulfil them; to give them a new content and meaning. They were to be neither simply 'structure' nor 'communitas' in place of structure: neither the Sadducee or Pharisee compliance with the status quo on the one hand nor the Zealot revolutionary society or closed purified community of the Essenes on the other.

The emerging structures of the New Testament Church, the Apostles and sub-apostolic leaders like Timothy or Titus, and the first forms of proclamation and teaching, of liturgy, creed and canon—all these came into being to sustain the community of love and shared forgiveness and to keep it open to all comers. Paul's missionary ventures in particular belong to both structure and community. Neither can wholly claim him to be his own. His calling came, as he firmly asserted, through no man, and there seems little doubt that the Spirit spoke to the Church at Antioch through Paul's own strong clear voice. Yet he was at pains to be sent out by that Church and to report back to it. Even when he felt driven to a new mission to the west, he would seem to have written to the most eminent Church there, that of Rome, in order partly to secure their support for the new move. Even later, when structure, institution for its own sake, threatened to stifle the Church's growth, renewal movements and revivals, varying types of covenanting community, have arisen in that strangest of all proofs of the reality of grace, the *ecclesisa semper reformanda*, the Church always being reformed, its structure constantly stretched and strengthened by community to make room for the perennial freshness of the Spirit.

Structure needs community
Recently, Ralph Winter, one of the Pasadena church growth school, has echoed something of Dillistone's argument when he claims: 'Every Christian tradition, whether Protestant, Mennonite or Roman, in so far as it depends upon a family inheritance or ... a biological mechanism for its perpetuation over a period of time, will gradually lose the spiritual vitality with which it may have begun.' He sees that, whereas the Roman Catholic tradition could make up for this loss by creating new 'orders', the Protestants could only resort either to throwing up new groupings, fragmenting into a myriad denominations, or to the acceptance of new 'para-church' informal agencies, like missionary societies. When these denominations or missionary societies become established and harden into new structure, fresh communities have to arise. Thus he points to the recent emergence in the States of large-scale groups of this kind such as 'Youth with a Mission' or 'Campus Crusade', with their tremendously

demanding and challenging appeal to the enthusiastic young whom they mobilise in their thousands.

But, unfortunately, these bodies often lack a positive relationship to the institutional Church. They become powerful, virtually independent, bodies which fail in accountability to the Church as a whole. What is needed is that such bodies should be linked firmly to particular Churches, as the Roman orders have always been to some extent at least. Even in the Middle Ages the Pope was approached by Francis of Assisi so that his new venture could be given papal blessing and, later, direction. Rome itself, for all the tension between order and diocese, knew how to use the orders in the service of the whole ramshackle structure of the Church.

Winter seems here to underestimate the tensions that have existed between orders and bishops. But he rightly affirms that non-Roman Churches need similar forms of community-societies that will have the same complementary relationship to their Churches. Only thus will the problem of the autonomous interdenominational agencies on the one hand, and the over-restricted and inward-looking local Churches on the other, be resolved.

Now there is much that is powerfully attractive in this argument, which seems to marry with what I have been saying about structure and community. Lesslie Newbigin, in his CMS sermon of 1978, rightly criticised Winter for talking of these denominational societies as a special élite on whom the rest of the Church must depend for growth. Bishop Newbigin felt strongly that such a notion of a 'mission' distinct from the local church and superior to it detracts dangerously from the life of the ordinary congregation. It is the local church that is the locus of the true evangelism of those who are attracted by the ordinary life, worship and witness of the Body. This is how the Church genuinely grows.

Newbigin is properly hostile to the idea of an élite. It is true that Roman Catholic orders and Protestant missionary societies have alike been responsible for propagating a notion of a first-class spiritual citizenry of some kind. The monks and nuns, the 'religious' (a give-away title), tended also to be seen by the faithful in the Roman Church as *the* missionaries. Similarly their Protestant counterparts have been put on a pedestal in a Church whose main function, as its whole structure and system of clergy-training makes clear, has become pastoral rather than missionary, moulded by a static maintenance model.

But once take a more post-Vatican II theology of the Church and of monastic orders seriously, and the objection somewhat fades. In the new picture of the Church, mission is seen clearly as the task of the whole Body. The bishops are to be the chief missionaries. The emphasis is on the Church as a whole. The missionary order or society is simply one manifestation of that Church alongside others. It becomes one expression and instrument of a missionary spirit which exists in the local churches and in the Church universal. The society becomes a kind of sign or sacrament of the Church as a whole, just as the Church is a sign or sacrament of the coming kingdom-community. The society by the particular commitment and dedication of its members should point the local church itself to its own essential character as a committed community.

The voluntary society, like the order, becomes the servant of the local church, standing for and embodying the openness of that church to the kingdom. And international fellowships and teams of dedicated people must seek to witness to the true nature both of the Gospel and of the Church which they go out to bring to life and, in unevangelised areas, to bring into being. Indeed, for a recent Benedictine study of monastic life, 'the meaning of monasticism is to be sought in the centre rather than on the periphery of the Church's life'. The Church needs such communities, not to live its life for it, but to show how it should be living that life and to encourage it so to live. Orders, missionary fellowships or whatever it may be, can foster the renewal of local congregations and encourage cross-cultural mission. They will provide one means among many others. Sometimes, reciprocally, they may themselves receive powerful stimulus and reinvigoration from the local church.

Now is the time across the whole Anglican Communion for this emphasis on 'covenant communities' to be re-inforced. The present centralisation of mission in the diocese and in the province is no guarantee that mission itself remains central. Quite the reverse. In Partners in Mission discussions the maintenance and development of the existing structure have tended to bulk larger than outreach. Yet never was there a moment when the Church needed more to get out from under its institutional encumbrances, a fact which a younger generation all over the world would seem to recognise all too impatiently.

The present evangelistic opportunity, the needs of the surrounding world, the pressures of world-wide poverty and injustice, the universal hunger for direction and meaning, all demand a total transformation of the Church. They demand vigorous lay participation, a new quality of compassion and of evangelistic witness, a readiness on the part of every one of us to attempt to move across cultural frontiers. All our church structures must now be judged, in Ross Kinsler's words, 'by their effectiveness in allowing and enabling people themselves to discover and express their faith'.

For such a purpose, special 'ginger' groups are needed as much now as ever they have been. Groups which, like the early evangelicals of the eighteenth century, like the Clapham Sect, like Charles Simeon's young men, like the Tractarian priests in London's dockland in the later nineteenth century, will discover special bonds and special spiritual resources for special tasks. Alongside the movement of Partners in Mission and provincial centralisation we need in the Church, as in secular organisations, a deliberate 'un-coupling' of the system so that the centre serves not to direct but to co-ordinate a multitude of varied initiatives. We need to see the Church, like society itself, becoming something more of a 'community of communities' in which congregations, cells, teams, societies, orders of all shapes and sizes, share in a worldwide movement of prayer, witness and service.

The summons to a genuine mission among the poor of the world, which was voiced at the World Council of Churches' Conference at Melbourne, may well be served best by such a development. Raymond Fung in Hong Kong, Joao Libanio in Brazil, others working in inner-city Britain, have exemplified the role that missionary incomers can fulfil by sharing in a team with local Christians and helping to stimulate and bring into being the basic communities, the cell groups, by which alone the vast urban wastelands of new Third World towns and decaying western inner cities can be won for Christ.

In East Africa, even in the rapidly expanding Churches of Kenya and Tanzania, in West Africa, in the Churches of Nigeria and Sierra Leone, in North and South India, as much as in Britain and other parts of the West, a younger generation is impatient and restive with the heavy inherited forms of worship and organisation. There is a real danger of much of that generation's enthusiasm and energy being lost to the Church and diverted to 'para-church' gatherings or breakaway groups in growing numbers. A cry has gone up to us from Uganda from a number of voices: 'Why not internationalise CMS?'

While it might not be right to impose a western pattern on other areas, there is no doubt that encouragement and scope could be given in many a diocese and province to harness the enthusiasm and organising ability of laity and younger clergy who might come together to create their own voluntary movements. In some Churches the leaders have shown the way. Bishop Wickremesinghe of Kurunagala, Sri Lanka, has lent special support to the Christian Workers' Fellowship among the tea-workers and to Arnold Mendis's inspiring Ceylon Inland Mission, both autonomous missionary ventures. In Bangladesh a tiny Bengali sisterhood, a potential successor to the Oxford Mission, is flowering if not yet spreading. Partnership in Mission, formerly a North American missionary body, has now reconstituted itself as a kind of international missionary order led from a base in Mexico.

Recently Theodore Williams has drawn attention to the rise of a mass of indigenous missionary movements in Asia, Africa and Latin America. In India, the Mar Thoma Syrian Church's evangelistic association (1888) and the Indian Missionary Society (1903), followed by the National Missionary Society (1905), were pioneers. But in the 1960s and 1970s the movement took off in earnest with a whole cluster of societies in Japan, Hong Kong, Taiwan, the Philippines, Korea, Indonesia and twenty or more in India, and with larger associations of such missions forming. In Kenya, diocesan missionary associations, admittedly closely tied to the diocesan structure, are supporting missionaries in their own area, while a newly formed overseas mission board (again a model that suggests almost too much central direction) intends to send Kenyan missionaries overseas. Similarly, in West Africa, the Evangelical Missionary Society, the missionary arm of its parent Church, has sent 200 missionary couples to the Maguzawa and Fulani people in the north of Nigeria, as well as to Ghana.

In Latin America, Pentecostal and other Protestant groups have sent out missionaries from their own to other areas, notably the Brazilian Baptists and Assemblies of God. Williams points out the advantages enjoyed by missionaries sent out by a relatively poorer Church in 'a mission out of poverty', as he calls it, rather than of affluence. Juan Carlos Ortiz's church sent three missionary couples to another part of Latin America with three months' support and a one-way ticket. They were to support themselves thereafter until the Church that sprang from their labours was able to take them on. It would be easier for such relatively 'powerless' missionaries to identify with the poor and oppressed, like the early Christian missionary movement. How desperately western missionary agencies need the stimulus, the corrective, and the restoring of their own integrity which a genuinely inter-dependent partnership with such Third World groups could give them.

Equally, however, Williams also points to problems faced

by such enterprises, lacking often not only the organisational resources, the training, the experience, of western agencies, but also the perception of what such missionary enterprise might entail. One Korean missionary, Chung Chae Ok, has written feelingly of the need for more understanding support than she received. Both she and Williams indicate clearly the need for co-operation with the existing western movement, for a sharing of staff, finance and information, a real partnership in trust.

Many of these ventures are still interdenominational; none is Anglican. Surely the moment has come for the engendering of such bodies within the Anglican Communion itself. Indeed, might it not be possible before too long to contemplate forming a federation of such agencies worldwide, at the very least within a certain group of Churches with common links? Could we not arrive internationally at something akin to the denominational society to which Ralph Winter gives such particular emphasis?

Community needs structure

And surely this stress on a proper relationship with an existing Church is also wise. A community movement that breaks away entirely from the structures and becomes a detached organisation on its own can often grow into a formidable structure itself. The whole theology of the Church of England's Partnership for World Mission was an attempt to develop a healthier relationship between autonomous groups and a synodical Church. But many an 'undenominational' movement, from house-churches to major international bodies, has become a newly dominant structure in its own right. In the house-church this can mean the reign of one particularly powerful personality. In the international body it implies a dangerous lack of accountability to any one church centre or of responsibility to the local Church. The statement of the recent Conference on World Evangelisation in Thailand drew specific attention to these dangers.

In a striking paper on the perils of such western

missionary bodies, Vinay Samuel and Chris Sugden compare them to multinational business corporations. They point to some disturbing analogies. Western-based global organisations can trample into sensitive areas in the Third World promoting a detached verbal message, intended to be as widely distributed by methods as ruthlessly efficient as the inappropriate products of some powerful commercial multinationals. Their product, a 'gospel message', so-called, which is as unrelated to local needs or situations as baby milk or special beverages, creates its own agencies and artificial responses. Such bodies tend to work, the paper suggests, through their own subsidiaries, which are judged entirely by their capacity to distribute an identical product. 'If the national Church is not an effective distribution centre for the product ... then it is bypassed. The agency creates its own Church, its own distribution centre and will continue to do so.' Thus they classify the rallies, conventions and conferences by means of which such agencies create their own new patterns of dependence and 'build their own structures of fellowship and witness to meet the needs their non-incarnate gospel defines'.

The paper analyses the mechanisms, high salaries, new seminaries, new detached leadership with no accountability to the Church in the country, by which these 'evangelistic pirates' gradually move in on the local 'markets', throwing them into confusion. It adds a shrewd critique of their way of evaluating their 'profits and sales'. But its central point is that such agencies have no incarnational witness, even in their countries of origin, let alone in the localities in which they operate elsewhere. Their very 'market research' is carried out in places where they have no involvement in the struggles of their own society. Their gospel is wholly spiritualised, individualistic, disembodied. And 'a non-incarnational gospel necessarily will bypass the expression of an incarnate gospel, the national Church'. Samuel, Sugden and others are setting up a local fellowship with the avowed aim of combatting such a diversion of energy and of being committed to the strengthening and renewing of the local Church.

No voluntary group today should seek to exercise power without responsibility. Those who seek genuine community must also relate to existing structures. Both Ralph Winter and Donald McGavran have tended to see 'frontier mission', as they call it, as an alternative to 'inter-Church aid'. Winter still talks of what he calls 'first-stage activity' in mission—that is, primary evangelism and the crossing of major geographical or cultural frontiers—as preliminary to what he describes as the second stage, 'interchurch partnership in mission'.

Now this seems to be putting the whole process precisely the wrong way round. The first stage is manifestly where we are beginning to be now, that in which the western Church seeks sensitively and penitently a new self-critical relationship of genuine partnership and trust with its Third World counterparts. This inter-Church relationship is primary, in a way with which Pasadena, it sometimes seems, has not yet wholly come to terms. Indeed, all western Churches, societies, orders, movements, still have some way to go in working this through. There is a danger that the Edinburgh 1980 World Consultation in Frontier Missions, with its deliberate echoes of Edinburgh 1910, might be no more than a pious anachronism. The test will be whether it enables powerful western mission agencies to hear and respond to a possibly painful Third World critique of much of their present structures and modes of operation.

But the second stage, about to begin, will surely see a new type of international frontier mission emerging, in which the western societies and Churches, no longer dominant, still provide something of the finance, the infrastructure, the organisation and some of the participants. The Third World Churches will provide much of the leadership. Teams, part international, part local, shared initiatives, joint training and evaluation, will be launched from bases not necessarily in the West. The participants will be ready, above all, at whatever cost, to incarnate the gospel they seek to convey. a gospel which necessarily carries with it profound social and political implications.

Here is no divide between institutional Church and voluntary community. The instrument may well be a new international partnership of voluntary groupings sprouting from within many varied Churches. The institutional Churches from which such groups arise and in the areas to which they go will be ready to authenticate and to 'earth' them by their encouragement and support. Similarly the Churches which such groups help to bring into being will in turn free their own members to form such special communities. Between orders or societies and Churches there can then be internationally a reciprocal sense of responsibility and of mutual communication. The structures facilitate the spread of new community ventures. The communities stimulate and inspire the structures. In Christ they both need and serve each other.

An international movement
Already one group which is energetically active in planting churches and evangelising in the multiracial inner cities of Britain is making its own plans with linked members of Churches in other parts of the world, to recruit workers from overseas to come to work with it. The Interchange Scheme within CMS itself is just getting under way, and more missionaries are coming to Britain from parts of Africa and Asia. It is becoming more and more imperative that every member of CMS should be committed on home ground to some definitive cross-cultural involvement, some small piece of long-term loving and serving which involves both the crossing of some kind of social or racial barrier in friendship and the commitment of the time and energy that such friendship requires.

Increasingly our own Field Staff in Britain have themselves to become resource people, trainers for those involved in this kind of discipleship. The test of local CMS Associations may well become how deeply they are involved in such local activity. The test of our service to them will become increasingly how far they are able to make links between such involvement and similar ventures in which other members, including the missionaries of the Society, are involved in other parts of the world.

Even if CMS itself is not formally internationalised, in the next phase it must be our hope to see it as part of an international voluntary movement. Within this movement we would hope to see an increasing flow of workers from Churches in all countries, moving from one area to another as part of an international task force. The young of all ages in every Church could be summoned to share in such a movement of evangelism in a context of service and of identification with others, especially with the growing Churches of the poor.

The next step will be not only to reorganise such groupings as CMS internally but to prepare for them to mesh in to a wider international network. Meanwhile, we must encourage and invite the leaders of Churches around the world to encourage voluntary initiatives, to give their blessing and backing to movements initiated and led by lay people or younger clergy, and to be prepared to view with sympathy—indeed, with enthusiasm—the emergence of a new international voluntary missionary movement with its roots deeply embedded both in the Third World and in the local Church.

Recommended reading

V. W. Turner, *The Ritual Process* (Routledge & Kegan Paul, 1969).

David Rees and others, *Consider your Call: a Theology of Monastic Life Today* (SPCK, 1978).

Waldron Scott (ed.), *Serving our Generation: Evangelical Strategies for the Eighties* (World Evangelical Fellowship, Colorado Springs, 1980).

Lesslie Newbigin, *Context and Conversion* (CMS Annual Sermon, 1978).

Ralph D. Winter, 'Protestant Missionary Societies: the American Experience' in *Missiology* Vol. VII no. 2, April 1979.

The Form of a Servant

The lost dimension
It is encouraging to find Christians in many different parts of the world rediscovering one dimension of their message which we seem so widely to have lost. The kingdom community was the implicit theme of Jesus' teaching. His death and resurrection and the sending of the Spirit brought it finally into being. It became the essential medium through which alone the 'good news of Jesus Christ' could be adequately transmitted. From the outset this community had the characteristic marks which Jesus gave to it, namely: forgiveness and mutual forgivingness; indiscriminating openness and love for enemies in contrast with, say, the Dead Sea Scrolls community; sharing and mutual caring, with a special priority given to the weakest, the humblest and the poorest; a common life in which the gifts of each person are released and the demands of justice clearly exceeded; and a leadership which does not in any way 'lord it' but exists solely to serve and build up 'the Body', the least being greatest and the chief being servant of all. We are only just beginning to see how far the absence of this kind of shared life and witness, shaped by the gospel, limits and distorts our whole attempt to communicate our message.

The form of a servant
It was a great privilege to be able to join in the discussions of the United Mission to Nepal—made up of many churches and mission agencies, CMS among them—when it sought to clarify its aims and priorities. It had arrived at

something of a critical turning point. Coming into being as it had in the 1950s, its activities were naturally dominated in their original form by the way in which development was seen then. The emphasis was on individual witness to the gospel on the one hand, while no actual evangelism was allowed, and on the other hand it was on the economic aspects of development: trying to build up prosperity, creating an infrastructure, bringing technological and economic know-how in from outside and, with it, considerable financial investment.

Development projects were in general seen as essentially gifts from above, from outside, still somewhat imposed and intruded upon the poor who were to a large extent to be passive recipients. Resources flowed in to recipient countries on a relatively large scale accompanied by technological experts. Projects sprang into being, bringing with them people with a Western life-style and Western methods of budgeting and administration. It was essentially a project-and-technologically-centred approach which started with a particular interest in industrial engineering, a hydro-electric project, a technical institute or the development of agricultural equipment. Similarly, in health care the thought was that hospitals should be built and the (to us) conventional service supplied. There was less awareness then of the tension between the pressures implicit in such a process on the one hand and the underlying need for a more widespread, gradual, rural and agricultural, movement on the other.

This was not so much a clear and total witness to the full implications of the Christian gospel as something which grew up piecemeal in response to invitations from the governments or according to the particular professional predilections of the person who happened to be sent by a mission agency and to spot a particular apparent need. Outsiders came in in their numbers and power and impressiveness. Within the constraints applied by governments, they assumed authority to initiate change and build up a bureaucracy to administer the programmes.

The workers on these projects could demonstrate their

own individual faith, integrity and love, but somehow the
message which was coming across was an emphasis on
Western know-how, on hard work, production and commercial success, some kind of a work ethic rather than a
distinctively Christian willingness to accept failure and to
serve people fundamentally. The whole effort was
relatively individualistic and fragmentary, almost
opportunist. It carried with it a certain unconscious hang-
over from the traditionally charitable, ultimately
paternalistic, approach of missions in the past. Of course it
is good and necessary to work at an infrastructure in
countries so poor that they have little or none, and to
provide at least some kind of alternative technology. But
institutions and programmes are not in themselves
Christian because they are controlled, managed and
financed through a Christian mission.

In the Christian development world everywhere, the time
had come when it was really necessary to look hard at what
was the distinctive Christian message of the structure
itself. Did it fundamentally convey an impression of
spiritual resources or of material power? Was it something
true or alien to the gospel? Indeed, could missionaries
themselves be seen as unwitting accomplices in the serious
injustices in the countries in which they served? Was their
work in any way questioning existing political and
religious structures and values? Was it in any way tackling
unequal land-ownership, the domination by the urban élite
and of caste distinction and privilege, of traditional
attitudes and customs which prevented people from having
access to the means of production, and allowed for little
local sharing?

Pyramid upside down
Perhaps at no point has the United Mission demonstrated
its authentically Christian character more than in its
willingness to look critically at itself and to be open to new
possibilities. Many of those working within it, as well as
visitors from without, have long been coming to grips with
the kind of questions I have raised. Together they have

begun to catch the vision of a style of development which would point to the kingdom-community of the gospel. There has been about the discussion a quality of repentance and new expectation, a feeling towards new forms. The Mission has set out for itself a quite remarkable statement of purpose with an emphasis both on building community and on serving the poorest and most marginal in society in an integrated way which gives its whole work a new context and a new unity of theme. From the same impulse have sprung efforts to draw existing projects into this coherent pattern.

A hospital now being built becomes the base for a more widespread community health scheme. Indeed, a policy statement on health care recently made is a fitting model for Christian agencies and churches in other parts of the world. It roots its whole work in the training and fostering of village-level volunteers, and in the reinforcing of the existing National Health Plan in the direction of primary local health care. It commits the resources of the mission to giving clear priority to the needs of the poor in a way which will surely encourage those struggling for the same priorities within the government itself. Within such a scheme, where there are congregations empowered by the Spirit they could minister healing by both prayer and laying-on-of-hands, and so serve as participants in the whole wider scheme of health care. They would then demonstrate that the gospel they talk about is the motive force which unites a whole variety of forms of witness at different levels. Within such a wider frame the hospital base would come into its own, no longer as an isolated effort of a few individuals serving a restricted number of people, but as part of a coherent whole.

A hydro-electric project is in the same way to become the central theme of a whole range of local efforts at rural community service. You can similarly envisage the possibility of a large technological institute with its own linked workshops and companies, becoming much more than a separated effort serving its own purposes. It could lay the same emphasis as the health scheme on field workers in the villages, who themselves in turn would be living alongside local people long enough to win their trust, to learn and receive from them and with their help to find out the problems on which the skills of the institute could then be brought to bear. This is indeed to turn the whole pyramid on its head, so that in true kingdom-community style the villagers, and among them the poorest, are the central figures, and the structures and resource institutions will serve and respond to their needs in a way which must carry with it a radical challenge not only to their present social structure but also to our own!

Sitting with a member of the UMN who is a field-worker in a Nepal village, I could picture this inversion. He goes to the village to discover not just what *he* wants but what *they* want. His interest may be in bio-gas (gas made from manure) but there we learn more of their desire for an irrigation canal to stop land erosion when the river floods. The head-man's remarkable brother started a community group, the society 'with the little vision' helping the landless and providing services for the village. To him the kingdom-community—the gospel as my friend embodies it —makes sense. Together they draw on the help of a Japanese engineer from a nearby experimental farm, and construct a dam out of rocks with a steel cage. Incidentally a bio-gas pump becomes a possibility.

Instead of deciding on technologies which we want to develop, we have to respond to and serve people's requests and only then persuade them to listen to some of our ideas too, if they are appropriate! It is a relationship of equals. Professional instincts are kept in rein. The quest for 'my project', 'my programme', 'my power' has to go.

False models
Alas, the earlier western phase lasted for a long formative era in the history of the world church. Many new little Christian movements, like their more established neighbours, have been impressed with a falsely individualistic and ultimately competitive model of how to build the Church. After the first flush of enthusiasm for the gospel

they are soon, like Jesus' first disciples, submitted to the
same demonic temptation to power and self-assertion that
he himself faced with and for us. Western agencies flood in
with offers of financial help and material attractions from
supplies of free literature to trips abroad. The precarious
little movement can be shaken. Its leaders glimpse over
other shoulders great western-style budgets. Ideas of plant
and of institutions, buildings, printing presses and the like,
dependent on outside, become grandiose overnight. There
is mistrust of leaders and conflict between them. The first
love easily fades under the strain.

All this has happened before and CMS has unwittingly
played its part in it. The habit can still have us in thrall in
our own church, too often losing sight of the resources of
the Spirit in the Body of Christ truly rediscovered. The
churches in China or in Burma, the humbled Church in
Russia, the Kimbanguists with their five million in Zaïre
beyond, built up without a penny of outside help, have
much to teach us.

As T. V. Philp put it:

Man tries to climb up at the expense of the other and by
doing so he thinks he is reaching heaven. At the expense
of the poor, those who struggle and suffer, some
Christian leaders have tried to make and build a power so
that they can reach heaven. In this sense our theology of
liberation as much as our development theory can be a
jargon to fool others. Our trades unions and political
parties play the same game. They are all somehow, at the
expense of others, trying to reach heaven for themselves.

Indeed a number of spokesmen for the churches in India
have become increasingly critical of the way in which their
churches have been made so dependent on outside assist-
ance for their institutions by the very 'development model'
we implanted.

'I have not read,' Bishop Joshua of Bombay remarked
caustically in a letter to the same issue of the *North India
Churchman* in which T. V. Philp was quoted, 'of a single

Protestant missionary in India who came empty handed and started work budgeted on local resources. Nevertheless their work was good; it was good also in the eyes of our fathers who were converted. Now in the last two decades or so, when missionaries started pulling out, they left behind them a church structure and an institutional activity which do not reflect the image of the poor Christian masses. Had they been left to themselves there may have been a crumbling of structures and a humiliating 'come down' giving place to slow indigenous growth. However, this was not to be so ... During these ten years of the CNI we have been only increasing our liabilities in terms of structures, institutions, programmes and professional men, all of which are sustained by foreign aid—partnership indeed!'

We are left with the question as to what real 'partnership' means. How do those of us in the 'North' hand over resources which within the Body they owe to those in the 'South'? Surely it must be done through an agreed commitment to certain priorities. Such priorities themselves form part of the deepest obligation which Christians everywhere carry. That is the obligation to express faithfully, in being and action, the gospel of the kingdom in its kingdom-community fulness. We are, above all, called to witness to a pattern of corporate life which runs counter to the ways of this world.

The United Mission to Nepal will in due course hand over to the government the projects I have referred to. What must remain of its work, and of the work and witness of each and all of us, is the impact of a quality of community, forgiven, forgiving, undiscriminatingly loving, sharing and caring, cherishing the least most, so that the leader is servant of all. Such a community would so uplift its crucified Lord that those who see it would be drawn irresistibly to him!

Recommended reading
Nepal on the Potter's Wheel (pamphlet) United Mission to Nepal,
1970.
Commission on Institutional Implications in Health Care. *Final
Report 1979/80*, edited by Dr Sigrun Mogedal. (UMN, PO Box
126, Kathmandu, Nepal).
Partnership in Nepal, CMS film strip.

Way Through the Ways

Recently I was talking to an African friend, a former, or perhaps I should say a fulfilled, Muslim, for he is now a disciple of Christ. He was reflecting on his spiritual journey from a small village, which was still keeping to some of the practices of its ancient local religion; to the Islamic revival in the nearby town and membership of the Muslim Brotherhood; on, disenchanted, to work in the capital city where he fell in with a teacher of Sufist mysticism and, finally, to the little praying group of new Christians, many of them younger than himself, who were part of a fringe movement which has only arisen in the last few years. Here he felt that he had found at last the One who had been searching for him.

He told his story with the characteristically gentle dignity and courtesy which he had brought from his Islamic culture into the refining fire of his devotion to Christ. As he spoke, I was struck by the sudden familiarity of his story's central theme. There was something there which I had met in the testimonies of so many seekers—from Australian aborigine to Pakistani scholar, or from East African Nganga or healer to producer and ambulanceman in my own London suburb. Within each of them, often quite early on in their life, an inner gulf had opened up between intellect and imagination, reason and feeling. And there was a corresponding, parallel, breaking apart for them in the outer world, where the swift changing circumstances of surface life subject, as it seemed, to the play of material forces, appeared to outstrip all attempts to give them a meaning. There was an increasingly sharp discontinuity between ideal and hard reality, between divine and human, heaven and earth, as the spiritual realm faded into the realm of fantasy. And yet this left a gap which it seemed vital to seek to bridge.

Broken man for a broken world

My African friend's story illuminated the rich variety of ways in which people have tried to do just that—to span the gap between earth and heaven, between the surface world and some ultimate realm of meaning. But through the little Christian group he had met he stumbled, to his amazement, on a wholly new form—that of a broken man in the midst of a broken world; a presence in the midst of the divine absence; one who had crossed that great divide which separates our history from any eternal meaning; one who was to be found with us, alongside us, for us on this side of the gap. Here was the unmistakable sense of Divine Love, bridging the gulf between its eternal source and our very temporal, finite existence. Such a bridge was only made at the infinite cost of a fusion of justice and mercy, truth and compassion which could begin, through pain and emptiness and death, to gather up the tragic disintegration of our existence into some ultimate whole. here was a strange Divinity which did not seek from outside history to possess mediums who could manipulate the world, to inspire prophets who, by imposing the divine will in a visible moral triumph, could impose that will upon the world; nor to attract devotees who, having renounced the world, might seek to draw it after them.

The Christ who was disclosed in the little fringe group in the city had entered wholly and vulnerably into our life and death. He had established there the assurance of a divine forgiveness which does not by-pass our history in any way but rather moves through the midst of it. Thus, he released in the midst of our life a dynamic of forgiveness by means of which he could begin in us a breaking and a remaking. He could thus, as it were, take us into his death and his new life.

Entering into his death

Stories come in from all over the world of people who, in gradually increasing numbers, are finding this to be the only way left. They have made the archetypal Christian discovery that in Jesus forgiveness is the source of all we have. As they read the story and the words and call upon the name of Jesus, alone or together, and come to be baptised in that name, the 'Spirit of Jesus' (Acts 16:7) lays hold upon them and flows through them.

In the first instance, the Spirit enables us to begin to accept and to bear the pain of the great divide which runs through us and our whole universe. We are so deeply held in the divine love as to begin to let go the little self, the little, grasping aspect of our being, so as to find the true greater self, together with others 'in Christ'. This is part of 'taking up the cross', of losing life to find it, of being 'the seed that dies'. Indeed, it lies at the heart of martyrdom itself, as it did for Bonhoeffer from the start of his recognition that, in his *Cost of Discipleship*, 'when Jesus calls a man, he bids him come unto him and die'. Later he reinterpreted the idea less inwardly, as being wholly vulnerable, caught up into the sufferings of God through living fully exposed in this world; accepting Jesus's call to watch with him one hour.

In East Africa, surely it is significant that, at the crucial moment in the 1930s, revival came to black and white alike; to Joe Church and to Simeoni Nsibambi simultaneously at their famous meeting on Namirembe Hill. Both were feeling the closing-in of the grip of the whole secular transformation of their worlds. Joe Church came out of that new phase of the Holiness Movement which inspired the Christian Unions of the Oxford and Cambridge of his day. He was one of the whole sequence of Christian Seekers, Hudson Taylor and Temple Gairdner among them, who before and after him played their part in the two-centuries-long search for a deeper pervasion of God, a 'second blessing', a new wholeness in the face of the divisive power of an ever-increasing rationalist and materialist culture. Simeoni Nsibambi also had forerunners and contemporaries and followers in Asia and Africa. These, who were conscious of being interwoven for good or ill with the whites in the grip of the same social and cultural upheaval, sought to grasp and express aspects of the same message.

Many Christians in Japan, too, have been inspired by the call to enter into the fellowship of Christ's suffering and, in these and countless other instances in different parts of the world, Christians in younger churches have also been searching for 'the purgative way'. There are echoes here of the Desert Fathers fleeing the Church and the world of their day to arrive at the loss of the little angry, greedy, restless self and to find the new whole self. There are echoes, too, of a whole Eastern tradition today being revived in the varying forms of Mount Athos and the Coptic monasteries in Egypt, of those fleeing the worldliness of Byzantium, searching through the Jesus prayer for the way of forgiveness, of love, of humble service and the gift of tears, as prayer and faith move 'from the head to the heart'. There are resonances in modern times of the tradition of Mme Guyon and Fénélon.

But the central contribution of the East African Revival is surely its characteristically African corporate emphasis. There is the experience of an essentially shared humbling, a shared forgiveness. Each person in the body is ready both to challenge others to repentance and equally to be challenged. As the brokenness spreads through the body there is a quality here close to that of the 'Jesus' Family in China, as indeed of the method of training developed by Florence Allshorn for missionaries, a method taken up and developed more recently by George Verwer of Operation Mobilisation.

The social and political implications have never really been worked through as yet. The message of corporate repentance begins to impinge on tribe and race as when Joe Church and William Nagenda made their preaching tours in Kenya or when Joe visited South Africa. But there is still a vast untapped potential. There is a power of forgiveness which could influence and sustain politicians, civil servants and police. Indeed, it could itself be the motivating power of what Haddon Willmer has called the 'politics of forgiveness' pervading church and society with its implications of a social as well as an individual repentance, a confession of economic or political injustice as well as more private sin. In Christian Rural Service under Bishop Dick Lyth, forgiveness began to be a motivating and reorienting force in development. But here again, surely, wide implications for the world Church remain as yet unworked-out. We still await wholesale practical revival as we enter into Christ's death personally, corporately, socially and materially.

And risen life
Then, as the forgiveness flows through the corporate life, we find the need for a renewed sense of its power in the Spirit, to begin to go beyond acceptance of the divide, and the pain-bearing alone, the 'fellowship of his suffering'; to see these as only a part of a more positive and affirmative process, the 'power of his resurrection'. This is the beginning, even in this life and age, of healing and reintegration. It is still far from being all-forgiven and forgiving, but it marks a movement through 'the way of purgation', towards the ways of 'illumination and union'. The blood and the water flowing from the wounded side of Jesus can be seen as symbols of the Cross and the Spirit flowing through our whole being, individual and corporate. Jesus is seen, in the Johannine vision, not only as the Lamb of God who takes away the sin of the world but as the One who baptises (immerses) in Holy Spirit.

The promise of this profoundly healing, reintegrating power, an invitation to fulness of life, comes also, like the summons to 'brokenness' and 'death to self', as a message of encouragement, from the ancient Eastern Churches, from the indigenous pentecostal movements of Africa and Asia and Latin America, from contemplatives and charismatics, to the West. The charismatic renewal itself, the renewed hunger for contemplative prayer and the whole revival of the healing ministry of the Church are all signs of the beginning of a Western response. What we are still being challenged to explore, by and with the grass-roots communities of the Southern hemisphere—and Southern Europe—is a still fuller integrity.

A fresh inrush of the forgiving, searching and tender Spirit, which flows upon us through Christ, releases in us at unconscious as well as conscious levels a new realisation of prayer and worship—a river, a prayer of the heart into which we enter and which pervades our being. Here is the stillness, the *Silent Music* of which William Johnston has written, and the sound of praise. Here is the song of tongues freeing the all-controlling self-consciousness of Western man, and the Jesus prayer, the repeated phrase of infused contemplation, which gradually begins to pray itself through the rhythms of heart and lungs. The divisions in the heart begin to be healed; also the wounds of the past, the separation of assertive strength from hidden weakness, reason from emotion. We begin to be able again to think our feelings and feel our thoughts.

Once again the central pentecostal and charismatic contribution—more especially associated with West Africa rather than East, and with South America—is the corporate aspect of this healing life. There is an emphasis on the gift and the potential of each person and sometimes an awareness of an almost supersensory co-operative working. The diversity in unity brings out the balanced significance of individual and group, a crucial middle way between the rival collectivism and individualism of the West. The poorest, the weakest and the least are the most important. The humblest is the greatest of all. There are glimpses of the kingdom-community to which Jesus called his followers.

In many of these grass-roots communities there are clear social and political implications. The gifts are not seen as purely 'spiritual' but as equally practical and material. The healing comes about not only through particular miracles but through the whole health of corporate and personal life. Spiritual insights inform practical, material and social skills. Little co-operatives spring into being; rich and poor farmers help one another. The most diffident, the poorest and the least educated discover their resources in the Spirit and grow in confidence. In places where business people, administrators or politicians are part of such a congregation, their eyes are opened to *new ways* of working, new depths of caring, new organisation patterns. There is a feeling forward and outward towards that participatory, mutually sensitive, intuitively open quality in both institution and society which tends to reaffirm the value and the contribution of every part to the whole. Churches, cells, teams, communities becomes a quietly pervasive movement of faith active in love.

Transfiguration

But the real secret of this way, through the whole tangle of ways and paths held out to the seekers of today, is its holding together of these two aspects of experience, the ideal and the real; the glimpse of some distant spiritual whole and the pain of our complex and broken actuality; resurrection life and the suffering and death. In Christ, the love which grasps us holds these together in a testing encounter. It rejoices in the new age and yet still yearns and struggles for the transmutations of the old. Its prayer is always both an adoration, an exultation in God, and yet a deep longing and pleading and interceding. This is no road to utopia. It is a quiet pervasive work of forgiving love, individual and corporate, inner and outer, spiritual and material. There are no simple solutions, no sudden revolution which perfects everything, no short cuts through the frustration of human weakness and failure. This forgiveness of Christ is, after all, an experience of wholeness, not yet a vision of the whole.

But the disjunction of mind and heart begins to be healed. The new wholeness, the integrity of earth and heaven, begins to be felt. Those who let themselves be drawn further into this death and resurrection will find themselves in all their relationships, beginning to be built together into 'a habitation of God in the Spirit', developing steadily upward and outward into the full-grown humanity of the Heavenly Man.

Recommended reading
Morris Maddocks, *The Christian Healing Ministry* (London SPCK 1981).
Sebastian Moore, *The Fire and the Rose are One* (Darton Longman and Todd, 1980).
Kenneth Leech, *True Prayer: An Introduction to Christian Spirituality* (Sheldon Press, 1980).
Maurice Sinclair, *Green Finger of God* (Paternoster Press).

A Sign for All Faiths

A letter came to me from one of those seekers on the fringes of the church I have met so often on my travels in Asia and Africa. These people seem to live and have their being in the border areas where the Christian faith and some other faith overlap.

On the edge of the city
My mind went back to the conversation I had with the writer of this letter as we bumped along a suburban track near his home. How often pilgrims of the absolute, out of the heart of different cultures, seem to live on the edge of a city, where the first buildings rise out of the desert or the scrubland, or the farms of the bush. The very buildings round us were the harbingers of change. They were signs of the new material power of technology as much as the main road or the reckless traffic. My companion, an extraordinary person, as such pilgrims always are, was a motor mechanic. So often these seekers occupy 'modern' roles. They can be anything from a teacher to an airline worker, or a government agricultural officer.

This man was a self-taught thinker, again a common characteristic I realise, steeped in both the Qur'an and the Bible as well as much of the theology and thought of Islam and Christianity and a wide range of modern literature of all kinds. He had a searching imagination and intellect. People like him are the sensitive and astute indicators, the points to much that is going on in their society. They are the poets and prophets, responding to the subtlest seismic shifts in their environment.

The great thing, too, about this particular man, which he had in common with the others, was his courageous realism. He seemed so intensely human and vulnerable, stripped as it were of conventional assumptions and responses. We were driving along the edge of a world where human beings appear to have a greater control of their own life. In practice this makes their frustration with their society all the more intense. They have moved out of the 'ceremony of innocence'—the rooted traditional world of their childhood—into the hopes and disappointments, the conflicts and uncertainties, of city life.

In the West, those who cross over into Buddhism or Islam, say, often strike one as having in some way 'freaked out'. They seem to have dropped away into an alternative half-world which lets them off the hook of some of the complex pressures of today's reality. But what impressed me about people like the man of whom I have been speaking is that they are at least groping for a more realistic, a more potentially flexible and adaptable, way of grasping the new facets of their life. They wrestle with more of its ambiguities and contradictions as they confront what is somehow a more naked, unprotected human struggle, stripped of the routine responses and categories of the past. You could almost read this in the innocent shrewdness of his expression. A smile of a kind of tender irony would light up the rather grave and inquiring expression his face had most of the time.

'Now we are all really divided within,' he was saying I remember, 'divided between our sceptical reason and our feelings, our longing for meaning and truth. And the world seems to be as divided as we are ourselves.' The smile came as he glanced sideways at me. 'New wealth, Coca-Cola and airline advertisements, western films, new office blocks and hotels, air conditioning on the one hand. Price rises, the politics of greed. And on the other, prayers, fasts, feasts, appeals to the way of the Prophet, and, just to make sure, protective charms against the evil spirits.'

'In reality the fixed order of the past is fading and breaking up. Other explanations of things, other religions and ideologies, Marxism, above all science, begin to compete. There's a whole new emphasis on human power, human success, above all human *choice*. I like what Peter Berger says: "modernity is an expansion of the area of human life open to choices". Instinctively our people too begin to feel that.'

'Well then,' I asked, 'and how do you choose?' We stopped by the wall of his house and he looked at me.

'Well, of course, we choose in the same way as scientists choose. We have to choose what really fits best to life as we know it. Reading or listening to the radio or meeting someone from elsewhere like yourself may present us with many possible ways through the world; many pictures of God or of how life is. Of course our upbringing, our whole way of being, affect us too. So we're faced with competing theories, inspired visions or guesses, which different groups have developed. We're doing it all the time from our childhood, doing it with our senses, doing it as we learn a language; even more if we learn three languages as I had to. As one of your thinkers put it, we are like fishermen casting a net. And if the mesh is right, if the size is right and the place is right, then we bring in our haul.

'That's what I've been doing with a group of friends who talk and pray with me. We read the Gospel stories and the Qur'an together. Even scientists, you know, often start with a picture. What about that ...' he hesitated for a moment, 'that double helix you spoke about, the one the DNA molecule people began with?

'Well, we too have started from a new picture, "He that has seen me has seen the Father." Jesus was our picture, "the brightness of his glory and the express image of his power" ...' He almost chanted it. 'What opens up for us from him seems to us a correction and a fulfilment of what we knew in the Qur'an. It is the most comprehensive. It covers all our experience, old and new. It's the most coherent. It makes the most sense of our struggles in life. And it's the most fruitful. It leads to the most worth-while life; the greatest help with each day. So we have come to believe this and to trust him. Both.'

I asked why he couldn't, then, join the Church.

'One day we may have to. But it seems too broken up itself and divided in its vision. Our people get mixed up there.' He laughed. 'You see, the West is too analytic. We are too ... synthetic. You don't know how to read a story; we don't know how to reflect on it.' He said he was beginning to find a way through by reading the Russian novelists, especially Tolstoy and Dostoievsky.

'The old Russian spirit is different, it moves more, as you say, between East and West. One day we shall have a mission to your Churches to help you to recover the meaning of your faith.'

Freedom against order
That conversation and that encounter are two of many which have set me thinking and praying furiously.

What is the change in recent human experience to which these explorers on the frontiers of faith, like watchmen on the walls of the city, are more alert than the rest of us?

The conversation I have just tried to recall pointed to two features. Both are strikingly similar to those of which Peter Berger, one of the interpreters of this change, has written. One was the increase of choice. 'Modernity is pluralism,' as he puts it. The other was the immense increase in human control and autonomy. Berger quotes a pithy description of 'the measure of modernisation' as 'the ratio of inanimate to animate sources of power'.

How, then, have the traditional frameworks of faith survived this ever increasing process, especially in those cities which are its most dramatic product? It seems as if all of them, beginning with Christendom, have been falling apart into a continuing conflict between secular freedom on the one hand and a recurrent yearning for some kind of spiritual order and control on the other.

After all, the characteristic feature of most traditional societies, at least since humankind ceased to be wandering fruit-gatherers and hunters, has been some kind of fixed transcendent order underpinning a particular social order. Each has tended to influence the other.

Within such an order there is very little scope for a free play of either human or inanimate things, at least in theory. Though there is usually, interestingly enough, some kind of a spiritual underworld, as you might call it, which often copes with extraordinary changes or innovations. It tends to be developed by those members of the particular social order who are excluded from the centres of power, the non-conformists, relatively speaking. From among these from time to time, can arise a new spiritual and temporal power of some kind which may even become the dominant pattern of a new society.

But the main characteristic of the traditional world remains a fixed, transcendent order accounting for everything and everyone. The nature of the transcendent divine power varied according to the particular culture which it had helped to shape.

Let's look at just three patterns of transcendence.

First, there was that of some of the smaller-scale localised societies of sub-Saharan Africa. Here the whole social order and every happening were interpreted as the result of the activity of a remote, abstract, creator High God under whom a range of fixed spirits underpinned the community and its various segments. There were the clan Spirits and Founders, and the spirits and fathers of families. Over against these the underworld was provided by the spirits of the wild, or of the waters or whatever, from without, served often by women or younger men.

Second, the semitic, external God of Judaism, Islam and even, to some extent, of medieval Christendom. Under the influence of Greek philosophy at least he comes to be seen as the remote, self-sufficient First Mover from whom, indirectly, all other subordinate causes have their own movement. This picture yields a fixed, predetermined plan. Indeed, it is hard to see how a contingent world can even originate from such a necessary, self-sufficient Divine Being. The alternative here is perhaps provided by a mystical tradition, with a tendency to an Eastern-style monism, seen at its most extreme in Eckhardt. In Islam, this alternative takes the form of Sufi pantheism. There is also, in both Christendom and Islam, some kind of radical, apocalyptic alternative, whether it be the popular millenarian movements like the peasants' revolt, or, in Islam, Shi'a eschatology and revolutionary yearning.

Thirdly, the immanent, all-containing, all-absorbing Divine dimension of eastern religion. Here the created order is a kind of emanation, almost it could seem a decline or decay from within the heart of the Divine Being, though some strands of the tradition are more positive and see it as 'the Eternal Spirit's eternal pastime', the great dance. All unfolds from the fixed, self-sufficient, necessary One, and to that Unity all must strive to return. There is no room here either for freedom or contingency. The 'dharma', the law of being of each level of creature is fixed, and its degree of conformity to that law determines its 'karma' or destiny in its next existence. All steadily unfolds through the 'commonwealth of transmigration' through the innumerable lives through which each being must necessarily pass. The social order, of gods in their pantheons, and humans in their hierarchy of castes, likewise unfolds from the pure to the impure. Here the only alternative is provided by renouncers, spiritual leaders who break away outside the normal spiritual and social order to offer the possibility of some special means, through their particular cult and sect, of direct access to and union with the Divine.

Here, then, are three types of traditional fixed order. What happens to them when the great disruption of the scientific and technological revolution in the West comes?

In each case it would seem that the upheaval—which my friend on the edge of the city observed—creates the same kind of transformation. That is to say, the fixed order increasingly fades and disintegrates and the 'underworld' or alternative is left to try to take its places. This happens at varying pace and degree according to the depth of penetration of modernity. In the small-scale world described above, the new social mobility and the impact of forces from without weaken or annihilate the fixed spirits of clan and family. New free-ranging spirit cults rush in to seek to fill the gap. These may take the form of new cults or of 'independent churches', linking up with western movements. They may seek to monopolise the High God.

In Islam, as in Christendom, it was the link between the remote Deity and this world which became attenuated into what is called Deism. The deity is seen as something like a great clockmaker and lawgiver, who set the whole machine in motion and left it to run. Liberal commercial Islam and nominal Anglicanism are alike in the same kind of vaguely unitarian, rational faith. All this becomes increasingly faint and attenuated. The alternatives? In Christendom, romantic mysticism and pantheism or intense pietism. Even Marxism itself can be seen as a last, romantic attempt to preserve the unified order of a traditional type of society with an aura of science and modernity about it. In Islam, the Shi'a apocalyptic spirit seems to attempt a takeover, even in the former strongholds of Sunni orthodoxy. It can be argued that all Islamic revivalism, from the Wahhabi movement to all the numerous progeny of Al Afghani, have Shi'a roots. All that remains, then, are varities of Mahdist apocalyptic, such as we have seen in recent years in West Africa, and Sufi mysticism, also fashionable in the West, where all alternative half worlds meet!

In Eastern religion there has been a similar erosion of orthodoxy with its fixed spiritual and social order. Although the caste system will take a long time, it seems, to fade and is powerfully persistent even within the Christian Church, it certainly is changing. Meanwhile, Sanskrit orthodoxy seems increasingly rare. The pandits in Varanasi feel marooned in a lost world. It is once again the alternative, the renouncers, the gurus who have rushed in, and renounced literature like the *Bhagavad Gita*, itself not even part of the core of the original 'canon', which in modern translation has come in to take the centre of the stage.

Traditionally it used to be said that 'renouncers cannot return'. They were supposed to leave the normal social order, renounce their place at the hearth, and head for the Himalayas, like Kipling's Purun Bhagat. But almost the whole so-called Hindu renaissance, together with its populous foothills, the Sai Babas, Rajeeshes, Maharishis and the like, from the famous Swami Vivekenanda on, are would-be returned renouncers. Even Gandhi can be looked at in that light.

All this half world, then, linking up from its beginnings with that other romantic half world in the West, has rushed in to mingle with an intensely materialistic modernity, which jostles alongside it in cities, in festivals, in varying new cults, in exotic films.

So the gulf widens—the gulf between a necessary fixed transcendence, whether exclusive Islamic style or inclusive Hindu style, and the increasingly free and anarchic all-too-human and materialistic world of modernity everywhere. The same distintegration could be analysed in the much diminished Buddhist world. The same reasons could be adduced for the fashionable addiction to Buddhism in the West, and for its use by romantics there to attempt to reinterpret Christianity or even modern science itself in terms of Buddhism. The same account could be given of the rise of new religions in the materialistic Far East and of the success one or two of them have had in the West. All these are attempts to provide an alternative, unitive and ordered haven from the growing freedom and relativism spreading in the wake of science and technology and commerce.

All the time order is being eroded by freedom and contingency and seeming chaos, so fresh attempts are made to revive some form of traditional pattern of spiritual control. Marxism seems to offer the last available collective version of the 'counter-modern', an alternative world with a fixed order of enforced stabilised values, of hierarchy and mass unity. Alas, any such attempt at a necessary order must now have about it an ultimately sterile air of captivity.

A new love
But if the God of some traditional Christian philosophy can seem to be imprisoned within the necessary, rigidly-

total transcendence of Islam or Advaita Hinduism, mercifully the God who disclosed himself in Jesus Christ does not. The God of the Bible, of the Christian gospel and of the vision of Christian saints and reformers through the centuries does not. He presents us, in the face of Jesus Christ, with a very different picture of his glory. We can see him through the eyes of Julian of Norwich, say, or William Langland or of the unknown author of the first poem in English, as the wounded Creator of Blake's famous etching.

This truly living God is not bound in the fixed necessity of the logic of either Islam or Eastern religion. Rather, he holds together in one, at infinite cost, both justice and mercy, necessity and contingency, order and freedom. Here God is disclosed as a 'new Love' holding together both law and free play, the spiritual and the material. He is both beyond us and yet all pervading, supreme and yet, for the sake of a great good, willing to limit his own sovereignty and omniscience, to be vulnerable and responsive to his creatures.

This is the great attraction of the good news of Jesus as the Christ, today. It is the reason why he appeals to so many often isolated watchers and explorers and pioneers in the realm of the Spirit. You can see it in the stories of a large number of these trail-burners in both Asia and Africa. It is there in the story and writings of Sadhu Sundar Singh, in the novels of Ayako Miura, in the poems of Tilak, in Bilquis Sheikh's testimony, and in the letters and conversations from the heartlands of both Islam and Asian religion of which I have been a recipient, with many others engaged in this work.

What these witnesses find in Jesus is essentially a new love, in which that justice and mercy, beyondness and closeness, utter consistency to itself and yet freedom and openness to the novel, are marvellously combined and relate heaven and earth in a new way—but only through the infinite pain of God realised on the cross itself. This discovery drives them back to an agapeistic Johannine Christology rooted in the knowledge here disclosed that

'God is Love' and that this essential nature of God is here directly, accessibly and unmistakably present. He can only be with us and for us unmistakably and completely in this crucified One.

Here the seekers find a vision of God commensurate with the demands of this hour. This is the reason why a Muslim writer, Hassan Askari, has described the cross as 'a sign in the realm of the relationship of God and man for people of all faiths'. Here is the strongest claim, among all the visions and revelations of the world, to a divine involvement in human and earthly history. This is the reason why, in a new kind of post-industrial urbanised world with all its humanist turmoil, the gospel and vision of Christ crucified is 'an idea' or rather a disclosure whose hour has come.

This understanding of God shows him as essentially Love, a realistic love which risks and gives its all in a material creation, and in bearing with and seeking to overcome the tragic nature of that creation from the beginning. He brings into being the possibility of a freely participating community of autonomous beings made to be like himself and to share in his divine life. In realising this union of order and freedom in himself in the person of Christ, he opens up the possibility of order and freedom for his creatures.

The Holy Spirit is the continuing realisation of this possibility through Christ, 'the love of God shed abroad in our hearts'. In the New Testament there is such an identity here that in fact the Holy Spirit is never talked of in cosmic or universal terms in the loose style of some contemporary theology. He is always the 'Spirit of Christ'. If there is any universality in the New Testament it lies in the Logos, in Jesus himself, the very principle and theme of creation. The interaction which the Spirit comes through Christ to bring about is something very different, part of the whole crucial process of the interaction of the gospel with all humankind in history.

Interplay
This is where so much contemporary Christian theology and more particularly theology of 'other faiths', seems to have

got its essential message wrong. Of course historically all faiths, including much Christianity, are elements in a whole repertoire of human responses to God and to reality, arising out of a whole succession of social settings, patterns of life. They are part of the whole human exploration of existence at different levels and in varying contexts. Of course there are many different models of transcendence, each with some truth in it, each with its limitations and distortions. We need to be much more aware of the whole range because each has something vital to offer.

But within the whole process there has come a moment, 'a moment in time and yet out of time', a crux, literally, at which there is a new commandment and a disclosure of a new love, the same as that which was latent in many places from the beginning, and yet different. The Church is at the very least the grouping where, often on the fringes, there has been the possibility of the disclosure among human-kind, as among the first disciples, of this crucial transformation of all faiths and all adherents of faiths, from the beginning to the end of time. It is not only a question of a new relationship between God and the creation, although it is that. Through that new relationship there is a new understanding of the holding together of order and freedom, justice and mercy, necessity and contingency, power and vulnerability in God himself.

But there is also released in the Spirit, that flows distinctively from God *through* Christ, the continual possibility of this same holding together of these opposites in love between human beings. There is a new corporate model for society in which also order and freedom, control and liberty, corporate and individual, community and institutional structure are fused by the continual realisation of forgiveness, costly grace, and of mutual affirmation. So structures of relationship that are distorted within people, between people, and between people and their whole environment in the universe, are seen as open to healing in an unprecedented manner.

In the attenuated and rationalistic christologies of much

contemporary theology there is no hint of this kind of directly accessible embodiment of grace in Jesus. Perhaps the thinness of rationalistic theology reflects much of the pallor of the institutionalised life of the Church.

The theology of other faiths in, say, a document like the current BMU document *Towards a Theology for Inter-Faith Dialogue*, while surely right in much of its essential stance is still rooted in the static, comparative, laying alongside one another of different patterns. It still reflects a little the 'debilitating relativism' which Alan Race rightly suspects 'hovers over all theories of pluralism'; the transcendent void into which all theories of some kind of complementarity, ecumenism of faiths or ultimate essence within all faiths, eventually dwindle away. Even the evangelical theory of 'redemptive analogies', implicit in Don Richardson's *Peace Child* has its dangers.

None of these theories recognises sufficiently the simple apprehension of the spiritual explorers with whom I began. That is, that all the traditional patterns of transcendence and of society are broken. In this sense we are at the same point in our contemporary melting pot as were the writers of the New Testament. We need, have always needed, a vision transcending the broken patterns themselves, whether Eastern and mystical, as were the roots of Gnosis and neo-Platonism, or Semitic and prophetic; whether immanent and monist, or external and dualist, 'to the Jews a stumbling block and to the Greeks foolishness'. It is this sense of a *process* in world history, of the dynamics of a corporate human enterprise exploring a whole repertoire of patternings of the divine and being met in the great exchange of God's entry into history in Christ, which our theologies of faiths lack. We need to be brought back to Paul's speech at Athens in Acts 17:23–31, or to Hebrews 1:1,2 for this sense of the true interplay of God in Christ and of a new convergence.

Christianity has lost the gospel and the life of the Body of Christ within the culture and social orders of this world. It appears now Islamic, now Eastern, in form and content, and more recently, divided into rational and romantic or pietist, has spread this division throughout the world. But the true calling of Christians is to go out beyond the frontiers of what we have walled around as 'the Church' into a dynamic interaction with the spiritual quests of others, in the whole intermingling of cultures which increasingly characterises our time. There God in Christ in his fullness will only begin to be adequately disclosed to us and in us as we are made ready to receive him with and alongside seekers of all faiths. We shall be Peter with Cornelius all over again. As all the fixed patterns of our old religions and ideological patterns break up, we too must be watchmen on the walls looking for a new convergence on Christ and his Cross, latent in all today's broken worlds.

Certainly within the relationship between God and creation implicit in Christ, both science and democracy, as we now understand them, were nurtured. Who knows what future delicate inter-relations of order and freedom, what new models for corporate living, or attempted solutions for those intractable problems of social ethics and politics, national and global, may not yet lie hidden as treasures in Christ? These and much more may yet emerge, as the whole apprehension of Christ takes shape in the future among Muslims and Hindus, Buddhists and African religious movements, and as Christians themselves begin to understand at last, in repentance and humbling, so much more than ever they knew before of the meaning of the very message that was entrusted to them. As the voice of the Spirit said to the poet R. S. Thomas in a deserted moonlit church in Lleyn:

> ... In cities that
> have outgrown their promise people
> are becoming pilgrims
> again, if not in this place,
> then to the recreation of it
> in their own spirits. You must remain
> kneeling. ...

The vision of the crucified is dawning on the fringe of cities, of our unrenewed, seemingly unregenerate Churches, and of many cultures and faiths. It is dawning where, almost beyond the Church, new communities are struggling into being. The ultimate fruit of that vision of God in Christ truly appropriate to our time must be a vision of order *and* freedom, unity *in* diversity in God, as will both shape and be shaped by a new society. A freely discovered, freely shared order in liberty, and unity in diversity, will be our ultimate response, as all our partial patterns are brought together in Christ under the final and unending Mercy.

Recommended reading

Peter L. Berger, *The Heretical Imperative* (Collins, 1980).
Towards a Theology for Inter-Faith Dialogue (BMU, 1984).
Alan Race, *Christians and Religious Pluralism* (SCM Press, 1985).
Judith M. Brown, *Men and Gods in a Changing World* (SCM Press, 1980).
Keith Ward, *Rational Theology and the Creativity of God* (Blackwell, 1982).
R. S. Thomas, *Laboratories of the Spirit* (Macmillan, 1977).

For support of my assertions about the theology of the Holy Spirit in the New Testament see:
C. F. D. Moule, *The Holy Spirit* (Mowbray, 1978).

The New Love:
Christians Relating to Those of
Other Faiths—An Affirmation

It is all very well to talk about Christian faith and other faiths, but as soon as we begin to meet in friendship those of other faiths our preconceptions can be shaken. 'Should we even try to draw devout adherents of other faiths to Christ?' some people ask. 'I always thought Jesus was the only way but where are we now?' was the question of a devoted CMS member after meeting a devout Sikh girl. Some who have always supported missions far away find themselves perplexed when faced with the experience, so familiar to many Asian Christians, of being a minority among people of other faiths in their 'home' territory.

Most of us have been living a long time in the false strength of an insulated Christendom, shutting out distant others with their stereotypes. We have never known the experience of Christ of early Christian times, when his witnesses confessed him as the true 'Way through all the ways' in a world of 'gods many and lords many'. We have not shared the experience of Christian minorities in areas of the world dominated by other faiths, an experience that can teach us so much.

But those Christians who break beyond the fear or the complacency that inhibit so many of us, and really get to know their neighbours of other faiths, can experience a marvellous enrichment and a fresh understanding of their own faith as they move deeper into others' worlds. Two CMS mission partners in Britain, Roger and Pat Hooker living in Smethwick in Birmingham, are playing a part in this still small but exciting movement among Christians all over the world who seek, sometimes at grave cost and risk, to break through cultural barriers and to discern Christ through the eyes of others.

Pat Hooker tells striking stories of the experiences of British Christians drawn into such encounters. There was the village church in Worcestershire which, at Pat's suggestion, invited her to bring a party of Sikh families from the city for an unforgettable day in the country. A great tea-party culminated in a gathering in the church. An exchange visit is planned, involving the villagers in visiting the Sikhs and their Gurdwara (worship place). There was a group of Christian wives who, talking to a Sikh woman, discovered to their surprise, almost shock, her strong sense of the love of God. And there were the Sikh questioners who probed what Christians really meant by 'loving your enemies' in a way that showed what glaring discrepancies exist between Christian talk and practice in this crucial area.

This kind of give and take in Christ may be hard for those who feel most threatened by what seems alien to their own old home surroundings. But those among them who venture in faith and love into real meeting with, say, Asian neighbours, have been marvellously rewarded. I recall a little black and white prayer meeting in an inner city church. An elderly Afro-Caribbean Churchwarden prayed for such a love to flood through Christians, bringing humbling repentance to the proud and healing restoration to the voiceless *within* our Church itself, bringing us deep into touch with Muslim, Hindu and Sikh neighbours, bursting the bonds of suspicion and prejudice and drawing us all into a new relationship. His amazing prayer could begin to be fulfilled if more CMS members and mission partners were to risk, under the guidance of the Spirit of Christ, new encounters with those of other cultures in the Church and of other faiths beyond the church, multiplying friendships as Roger and Pat and many others are doing already.

I would like here to affirm some principles for those engaging in such a calling to have in mind and heart as they set out.

Our greatest obstacle ...
To discover Jesus Christ as Lord through his Spirit at work in our own lives is to be grasped afresh by a new love (Matthew 5:43–48; John 13:34–35, 15:12; 1 John 2:8; Romans 5:5; 1 Corinthians 13). This love humbles us and lifts us up. It is a death to our old grasping defensive ego and life to our new selves in Christ through a God-given stream of outgoing, forgiving, challenging but affirming *agape* love. It strips us of cultural pride, our unconscious racism, and all those defensive attitudes which are British and western rather than Christian. The Spirit of Christ enables us to listen, to learn, and to exercise what Toyotome, a Japanese evangelist, calls 'evangelism of the ear'. The Spirit enables us more and more to give ourselves in vulnerability and so more and more to receive ourselves back again in a new, shared, more vital form. This, no more and no less, is the Gospel of Incarnation, of Love embodied (Philippians 2:5–11, 3:7–9).

There is a new relationship between heaven and earth, between God and all creatures (John 1:14); and we are given power to become children of God (John 1:12–13). There is potentially available, released among us, an infinitely realistic, all-enduring love. Our ordinary little, weak, fitful, sinful life has been brought into union with the divine life. This in-fleshing of the divine love is the centre and point of balance of the universe. To Paul on Mars Hill it is the crisis point for all religions (Acts 17:30–31). In the synoptic Gospels, Jesus himself is the kingdom (*autobasileia*), or reign of God, into which through his death all can finally enter. In St John's Gospel, 'He that has seen me has seen the Father'. An everlastingly new way has opened up through which, as we go down with Jesus through the Cross, we can be drawn up into the eternal shared life of the Trinity, bringing with us everything else.

The Cross was the only way in which this seeming impossibility of the finite and the infinite becoming one, of God being revealed as God with us and for us, could be finally and fully expressed. It is painful when we find many points at which this new relationship of God and creation in Christ through his cross is *still* unacceptable to others. The truth remains to the Jews, and to all strongly mono-theistic moralistic religions such as Islam, a 'stumbling block', and to the Greeks, and to all that monist Eastern religion from which the Hellenism of St Paul's day emanated, 'foolishness' (1 Corinthians 1:22–24). The Divine truly becoming material and working fully through the broken-up history of our material world is still counter to the whole spiritualising tendency of eastern religion. God becoming vulnerable and both accepting and transfiguring evil, suffering and conflict, is inconsistent with both the Islamic vision and that of African and of small-scale religions, where all evil must be removed rather than transformed.

At this point, for many Christians real antagonsim can arise, intensified by the hurt caused by our past arrogance. In the face of fanatical religious enmity, whether in militant Christians, Muslims, or various kinds of national-istic faiths in Asia, our sense of obedience to Divine Love in Christ is put to the test. This Love becomes a judgment on ourselves and much of the Church throughout its history, but also on all hatred and violence in the name of the divine. Many Christians have real—and on one level well grounded—fears of Islam. But this is where steadfast 'love for enemies' is the only witness: 'the story [of God in Christ] is only safe in the custody of those for whom every antagonism is an opportunity. For that, precisely, is the heart of the story itself' (Kenneth Cragg, *The Call of the Minaret*, 1956, p 179).

And yet, alongside and within the darkness of hostility, those who continue humbly to explore the spiritual perceptions of their neighbours of other faiths will be rewarded by the emergence of surprising shafts of light within seemingly impenetrable structures. We shall find that, as among ourselves, the perceptions of some of our neighbours are shifting and changing under the impact of modernity. A new, more dynamic, urbanised, technological world is shaking all the old frameworks. All religions are being tested in the melting pot of modernity. While many appear to take refuge in a destructive fanaticism which is frightening, we shall find others who are feeling here and there towards a temporal as well as eternal God, a God involved more in struggle, pain and seeming chance, a God who meets us in the midst of our upheavals.

As all religious worlds, traditions and social patterns mingle there are signs, even in mutual borrowing, of their being more broken open to each other, at least in the ever-growing cities. And there are more 'seekers'. Many of these are young. In the West they have looked East. In the East they may look West, pick up any literature, turn mystical or secular and sceptical, or again humanist or Marxist and radical. The common factor is a hunger for meaning. In a cosmopolitan centre like Singapore many young Chinese turn to Christ because the city life so undermines their traditional world views.

And who knows how many among all faiths are driven at moments to throw themselves on the mercy of a half unknown God? Like Cornelius (Acts 10) they cast themselves on the mercy with a sincerity that shows and surely (as Sir Norman Anderson suggests) find themselves unbeknown at the foot of the Cross.

... is our greatest asset

In a time of change, western Christian theologians have been tempted to try to adapt their heritage by throwing out anything that does not appear at first to fit a modern, rational and relativist world. Prime targets are the Incarnation, incorporating the totality of divinity in the man Jesus, and his physical resurrection. You can end up with a Christianised Unitarianism, closer of course to philosophical Hinduism or Islam. This makes for a short cut into unity with all religions. It seems to make it easier to join in a common struggle for justice and peace, 'All

Faiths for One Race'. This is the way of John Hick and there are large traces of it in Alan Race's work. It seems attractive and reasonable as we draw nearer in friendship to those of others faiths. It takes the tension out of it. Why stress what has become an obstacle?

And yet, if what I have said about what is happening to all faiths is true, we may be in danger, for apparent short-term gain, of casting away the very asset which we and they most need and which all are half-consciously seeking now more than ever before—the God who in Jesus Christ is with us in the midst of material and social upheaval.

We must therefore explore more than ever God's love incarnate in Christ realised among us through the Spirit in the 'Body of Christ'. This Love takes us ever further into the Incarnate, the Crucified and only thus the Risen and triumphant Way, through waiting, praying, caring, accepting misunderstanding and hurt, through discovering the good in others and being enabled to learn and receive from them. This is the imperative of the Gospel for us all.

We must study and follow the insights of those pilgrims from other faiths to Christ. We must let Sundar Singh (whose words of judgment still burn the hearts of westernised Christians), Watchman Nee, Ayako Miura, Festo Kivengere, Bilquis Sheikh and many others, lead us back to the Christ we have lost in complacent, fearful, defensive isolation or aggression.

If we are prepared to give ourselves freely with those of another culture or faith, to lose our ego life to and for them, then the Spirit of Christ, the one who sheds his love abroad, will guide them and us as we ourselves pray and trust in him who was broken and remade in glory for the *whole* world.

We must be ready to discern the work of the demonic from the witness to the God and Father of Jesus both in their religion and in ours. We must also hear the searching criticisms and questions of Muslims, Jews and Hindus and hear what God is saying to us through them. Before God, our critics are our friends. The Assyrian is the rod of his anger. We have much to receive. We must be responsive to that mighty tide of gentle inexorable Love with all its judgment and fulfilment pressing today upon all faiths, on their forms and assertions, to draw humankind to himself.

Within the worlds of other faiths the watchers have seen Christ dawn on themselves afresh alongside those to whom they were sent, as Peter saw him with Cornelius. They have seen the future coming Christ of the Indian Road, the South African township, the Housing Estate, the Inner City, the struggling village, the base community. They have broken beyond a purely westernised understanding in order to receive back the Christ in whom Western patterns are reconciled with those eastern and African patterns which had seemed so hostile, the Christ in whom Heaven and Earth, East and West, North and South, meet.

For those Christians, then, who are confused and uncertain as they meet people of others faiths, and perhaps even find in them a goodness and truth which surprises them, here is the key. Let them be opened into a larger vision than ever before of God's Love in Christ. By his very wounds he may now be the only healer of an alien, disrupted world. They will find that he will illuminate their new friendships and conversations with his presence between them and these new neighbours.

'Look to him and be radiant.' In the end, whether his children will have it or not, what is good in all faiths will converge on him. What is distorted will be judged. It is enough for us by little acts of self-surrender and obedience, of genuine love and openness to *all* our neighbours to prepare a tiny bit of the way where he calls and empowers us so to do.

Recommended reading

Sir Norman Anderson, *Christianity and World Religions* (IVP, 1984).
Roger Hooker, *Voices of Varanasi* (CMS, 1979).
Christopher Lamb, *Belief in a Mixed Society* (Lion, 1985).

Kenneth Cragg, *The Call of the Minaret* (OUP, 1956).
Christopher Sugden, *Christ's Exclusive Claims and Inter-Faith Dialogue* (Grove Pastoral Series No 22, Grove Books, Nottingham, 1985).

No Other Name

All that I tried to express in my ten years of writing the
CMS news-letters, 1975–85, even at its most abstract, has
been earthed for me in innumerable encounters in different
parts of the world and in Britain itself.

'I am debtor to all, to all am I bounden . . .'—debtor to
many of you who read these words, to many others also of
whom I have tried to write and speak. I glimpse again,
rising up before the mind's eye, many varied faces; faces of
every form and colour set in utterly contrasted
surroundings; faces I remember with awe and delight; faces
here of a Church leader, there of a venturer on the fringe of
the Church and there again of someone struggling his or
her solitary way through the other faith worlds which are
changing as much as our own.

In all of these faces is reflected a strangely elusive
identity, what I have called a family likeness, a tune
transposed into a wide range of keys yet instantly
recognisable. All convey the unmistakably familiar sense
of a fusion of flesh and spirit, and a particular relatedness,
not only to the Spirit but in the Spirit, to themselves, to
others, to the world. It is the sense of a 'New Love'. It is a
love which is at once shrewdly sceptical and yet innocently
gentle. It is the only fully realistic love the world has ever
known, the only love that knows the world to its depths,
knows us ourselves for all that we are. It is the only love
that holds together, in time and in eternity, judgment and
mercy, and that thus can contain heaven and earth; the
only love that, having its source so evidently beyond us, is
equally evidently so profoundly and totally with us, within

us, among us, closer to us than our own breath. And thus it is the only fully and ultimately redemptive love, which not only affirms us in our infinitely rich and diverse creatureliness, but also wrestles with the divisions within and about us; with conflict and guilt, with pain and ambiguity, with all that alienates and separates us, with time and transience and death itself. This love, our source, our theme, our life and our goal, leaps out at me from those myriad remembered encounters.

> Christ in ten thousand places
> To the Father through the features of men's faces.

This love has surely convinced and convicted us that there is indeed:

No other name
'Salvation is in nobody else; for there is no other name under heaven given among men, by which we must be saved' (Acts 4:12). I have seen, as I have argued that, in society at large, whatever remnants of faith people hug to themselves in private, modern technological and social change, working through the great city centres of the coming world, is breaking up the old frameworks of faith. People will go on, in Africa and Asia and South America as in the 'North', attempting to create and hide within alternative worlds of faith and culture, old or new; in Islam, as in Hindu, Buddhist or Sikh nationalism, or in the militant would-be Christendom of some Phalangists in Lebanon, or the born-again movement in the States.

I now repeat that the westerners that I have known who became Muslims or Hindus, or members of African and Asian cults old or new, were manifestly fleeing into an alternative wholeness from the divisive effects of modernity in their own culture. Those who, from within Islam or Hinduism or African religions, were drawn in their pilgrimage to Christ, have again and again proved to be people who were actively seeking to grapple realistically, critically but also positively, with those divisions of modernity. They were genuinely trying to 'take hold of change', to accept and yet to resolve the conflict. They found in Christ crucified, in a way that Christians in the West are still often only beginning to find, 'one Mediator between God and human beings' . . . within a new secularised, humanised, vulnerable world.

When a modern, urban, scientific world presents us with humanity alone—free, autonomous and desperately responsible—and when the masses of the poor and the hungry press for a place for everyone; when both Marxism and capitalism alike are failing to bring the fulfilment they promised and lack a human face, only the release of a new love can save us. Only a battered and crucified God, with us and for us and alongside us, can save a reassertive Islam or Hinduism or Christendom from themselves. Suddenly there is only one place where divine and human, heaven and earth, the Spirit and the secular, idealism and materialism, romantic and rational, really meet. There is in many people, cells and groups a dawning form, closer sometimes beyond the Church than within it, of Christ himself, seen from within an Islamic or Hindu or African cultic consciousness, and recognised only then as the Servant-Lord of all.

No other message
Then indeed we are compelled to recognise the form that the message, the good news of Christ, *must* take. His new *agape* love *must* be, as in him so in his people, embodied, realised, lived out. If he is to be recognised as the one mediator between ideal and reality, the spiritual and the material, his love must be seen and felt and experienced as a love which integrates inner and outer with a rare healing, fetched fresh from his cross and breathing his risen life. Only the *whole* gospel, evangelical and personal, catholic, corporate and sacramental; pentecostal and charged with spiritual power; radical, costly and vulnerable in its call to discipleship; orthodox in its total worshipfulness, will convey this true mediation.

That is why we have sought to emphasise the three

overlapping circles of personal evangelism and individual witness; corporate and community renewal of the Church and its institutions, hospital or school, releasing the gifts of every member, especially the seemingly weakest or smallest; and the struggle for the justice/righteousness of God's Kingdom, and for new models of society based upon the Gospel.

We see the need to find fresh inspiration from the base communities of the Church all over the world, and especially from the churches of the persecuted and the poor. We see the need to struggle to transform and renew institutions so that they will serve true community. Realistic institutional structures must be held together with our yearning for ultimate 'communitas' while this age lasts. Christian disciples must be channels for the Divine Love, personally in their care for each individual entrusted to them, corporately in their common life and their joint service to others, and publicly and in society in their passionate commitment to justice, to peace, and to the cause of the disadvantaged, the deprived and the oppressed. They must be plunged deep into the search for new models for a genuinely egalitarian, post-industrial society.

Integrally Christian individuals and groups all over the world must become pointers to the One who alone can redeem both particular human beings and, at this critical juncture in its history, humanity itself. His realistic love alone, mediating between ideal community and social institutions, between heaven and earth, between private world and public world, will offer the foundation not only for a saved and healed individual life but for a freshly human, genuinely pluralist, society and world; if only we can be true to him.

No other medium
I have spoken of scattered groups and individuals. But no mere sect or para-church movement, however 'spiritual' and single-hearted, can be the medium for such a wholistic Gospel and message. As Christ holds together in his cross

heaven and earth, ideal and reality, so the Spirit that flows from him holds together ideal community and actual institutions.

Only the poor old battered, insulated, much-failing and fumbling institutional churches now planted in each continent can fulfil this task. From our first foundation we in CMS have had, by faith and by grace alone, to believe in the so-called 'main line' institutional church, even the Anglican church! We have seen ourselves, also an institution in urgent need of renewal, as survivors in the 'dry bones' department, believing that the Anglican Church, the United Churches we are privileged to be bound up with in Pakistan, Bangladesh and north and south India, and the ancient Churches of the Middle East, Ethiopia and South India, *can* be renewed and raised up by the Spirit of God to do what no other body, however fervent and dedicated, can do.

We have witnessed with joy that 'all over the world, the Spirit is moving'. We have seen signs of the wonderful change spear-headed by those in the Orders in the Roman Catholic Church. We have dared to believe that such changes and more, changes in hearts and lives, in worship, in corporate and social witness, can take place in the other churches. We pray and seek to be made, with other societies, a spearhead of such transformation in the Anglican Communion and the other churches with which we are linked.

If we ourselves can be changed by God's lively grace and made channels of his new love in Christ, how much more can anyone else anywhere be changed also. Through Church-to-Church relationships, through the cumbrous processes of Partners in Mission consultations and joint working, through diocesan and other links, the societies can become the means by which the full gospel fire can spread, in personal testimony, in mutual encouragement, in deep intercession, in a multitude of friendships, journeys and visits. Para-Church bodies, like house churches or indeed interdenominational agencies, aid agencies and the like, are vital auxiliaries. We must be open to them and we have need of them, but in the end it is the ordinary infantry, so to speak, the local cells, congregations, dioceses and the like that, united across the world, must be the base for the spreading of the fire of Christ, the New Love.

No other method
And for this to happen truly we need each other across the world. We need each other's prayers. We need each other's insights. We need an exchange of stories and testimonies. We need, above all, participation in each other's mission. We need international teams, little communities like the cells of Taizé or of the brothers and sisters of Jesus in the slums, in the poorest villages, in the inner city, the housing estates, the tower blocks, the squatters' settlements. Above all, we need an exchange of people committed to mission, seeking to live out the New Love of God through Christ in the Spirit. Where he is lifted up truly he will draw all to him. We must witness to him as the Mediator between North and South, East and West, in whose Cross all barriers of culture are broken through to release a vital interplay of gifts and insights.

The toughest challenges to all committed Christians in this country are to participate in the mission of churches elsewhere in the world—at least for two years, sometimes for longer—and equally to receive Christians from elsewhere into our mission. Our own Church is rarely engaged in any very definite mission and that is partly why churches here cannot see how to receive and use the help of Christians from elsewhere. Where the new fire is burning, where there is mission, we shall know our need for each other, world-wide and indeed within this country. A true parity of interchange with churches in Asia, Africa and Latin America, and a true exchange between social and ethnic groupings and rural, suburban and inner-urban areas in Britain, may well be the next push forward. May I be privileged yet to be involved in this in the future.

No other means
For the sustaining of such a vision, for the exchange of people world wide and within Britain, for the spearheading of

transformation, personal, corporate and social, I believe we need, in the Church as in society, communities like Lee Abbey or Scargill or indeed Taizé; fellowships or so-called voluntary societies, provided they work closely, as a resource and a stimulus, within the wider synodical and diocesan church. In Christ structure and community, church and sect, are fused into one.

Indeed two things are required of every Church member, two threads must be woven through the consciousness of every congregation, both of which have run through much that I have tried to say.

The first is a growing, personal awareness of the presence and love of God *in* Christ, closer to each of us than breathing, through the Spirit 'poured out in our hearts'. That inner candle must be lit and re-lit every morning and evening as our prayer deepens and our love grows a little. It is this inward discovery of His constant forgiveness and fresh release of His *agape* love that we are to draw others to discover and come to know.

The second is a continual consciousness of the feelings and needs of others right outside or on the fringes of the Church. If you go and talk to them and listen to them you will soon hear what they think of the Church itself; what they resent and reject; what they long for, why they so often feel estranged. In the places of work and of unemployment and search for work, many people seem far distanced from all I have written of. And yet, they are near.

Very small changes, very small movements and gestures of welcome and openness, of listening of regret and sorrow, and trying to understand, would make so vast a difference.

When the Church seems simpler, freer, more open and accessible; even more, when Christians are more quickly and sensitively alongside others in all their needs and struggles; when faith-love flowing from its constant, inward source in Christ, transfigures our relationships in the world, drawing us truly together but also driving us out amongst those around us, then they will come. Many will come 'from East and West and North and South' to sit down with us in the Kingdom. They will come almost without knowing why they come, but sensing something of the summons of the One to whom they are being attracted.

Advent and Christmas bring us back to our beginnings. We may find ourselves kneeling in tears of repentance at the manger before the judgment and tenderness of that strange love 'Terrible as an army with banners'. We may find ourselves crying out with a longing that we may be enfolded in that love, that we may put on that 'shirt of flame', that we may draw others, indeed draw *all* things, to him. We find ourselves crying out 'If only we in the Church, in the midst of our world, could start all over again'. And then, as we kneel there dumb and broken, we shall be filled with a strange joy because out of his ever-glorious, ever-undying radiance we shall be enabled to hear his answer 'You can'. 'Behold! I make all things new. . . .'

Recommended reading
Jocelyn Murray, *Proclaim the Good News* (Hodder & Stoughton, 1985).
Kenneth Leech, *True God* (Sheldon Press, 1984).

TWO MILLION SILENT KILLINGS: the Truth about Abortion

Dr Margaret White

Essential, informed reading for all Christians on this critical contemporary issue; likely to engender wholehearted and healthy controversy.

GP Margaret White exposes the deliberate attempt to confuse the public over the issue of abortion by the use of euphemistic language and the minimizing of its harmful side-effects. She traces the history of abortion from legal, medical and religious perspectives, describes the clinical methods used to terminate pregnancies, and answers the various arguments put forward by the pro-abortionists in terms of God's basic rules for life. At the heart of these is the Creator's desire for his creation's health, stability and well-being. Dr White demonstrates that the extent of the damaging effects of abortion on women and society is one of today's best-kept secrets.

THE GOSPEL COMMUNITY

John Tiller

An important and timely call to the established churches to rediscover the distinctive life of the Spirit and to become true 'gospel communities' – attractive, authoritative and relevant.

Neither the experience of renewal nor nationwide evangelistic missions resulted in a mass return to the churches. Instead, the house church seems to promise a better future for Christianity. Can revival still come through the established churches? John Tiller, Chancellor and Canon Residentiary of Hereford Cathedral, looks at Jesus' radical definitions of the temple, priesthood and sacrifice, and outlines the style of leadership which will enable the church to become again a 'living temple'. A critical book practically showing the way ahead for the established church.

CHOICES . . . CHANGES

Joni Eareckson Tada

Joni has inspired millions with her courage and faith in dealing with her quadriplegia. In her third book, she writes revealingly of her life, her ministry and her marriage. 'I've sat in on bridal showers for so many others; it seems odd that it should be my turn. In my wheelchair with its dusty gears and squeaky belts, I seem slightly out of place among the delicately wrapped gifts and dainty finger sandwiches.'

This warm, honest, sometimes funny and often poignant autobiography shows us vividly that though life is full of changes – wanted and unwanted – God uses each one of them to make us more like Him. Illustrated.

EYES THAT SEE: The Spiritual Gift of Discernment

Douglas McBain

The first of a new series, Renewal Issues in the Church, which examines the effects of charismatic renewal on corporate church life and individual Christian experience from a biblical perspective.

Douglas McBain, a leading figure in renewal first in the Baptist Church and now on a wider basis, provides a comprehensive and thorough scripture-based guide to the gift of discernment; which, with the resurgence of emphasis on signs and wonders, healing and deliverance, is 'the most necessary gift for the present day church'.

If you wish to receive *regular information* about *new books*, please send your name and address to:

London Bible Warehouse
PO Box 123
Basingstoke
Hants RG23 7NL

Name..

Address ....

....

....

....

I am especially interested in:
☐ Biographies
☐ Fiction
☐ Christian living
☐ Issue related books
☐ Academic books
☐ Bible study aids
☐ Children's books
☐ Music
☐ Other subjects